MOSQUITO ATTACK!

A NORWEGIAN RAF PILOT AT WAR

MOSQUITO ATTACK!

A NORWEGIAN RAF PILOT AT WAR

TOR IDAR LARSEN

AND

FINN ERIKSRUD

FONTHILL

Fonthill Media Limited
Fonthill Media LLC
www.fonthillmedia.com
office@fonthillmedia.com

First published in the United Kingdom and the United States of America 2015

British Library Cataloguing in Publication Data:
A catalogue record for this book is available from the British Library

Typeset in 10pt on 13pt Sabon
Printed and bound by CPI Group (UK) Ltd, Croydon, CR0 4YY

CONTENTS

The book is dedicated to the memory of four brave, young men. Three of them were Finn Eriksrud's close friends, and gave their lives for our freedom. The fourth was a friend of mine, who lost his life in a Yak-52 close to North Weald Airfield, Essex, on 29 April 2014.

Gunnar Høverstad, Harold Odman, Andreas Wyller, and Simon Chamberlain.

Introduction

This is the fruit of the efforts of two young men living in very different times. Finn Eriksrud wrote his memoirs of the Second World War as early as 1945—he was 23 years old when he began, and had published them within a year. He was a Mosquito pilot, and the sole survivor of No. 333 Squadron's initial B-Flight detachment, based at Leuchars in Scotland. The flight suffered such terrible losses in its first year of activity that it was forced to halt operations in September 1943, for lack of pilots and training. By that time, Finn Eriksrud and his navigator Erling Victor Johanssen were the only crew left of the original flight.

The other author is yours truly, Tor Idar Larsen. I am 34 years old, over a decade older than Eriksrud was when he put pen to paper. Despite his youth, he had been through more than what anyone would expect of one life time. He was 18 years old when he escaped Norway and left his education behind. He experienced the occupation of his home country, two risky attempts at escape, and a journey that took him around the world. He trained to become a pilot in Canada before even reaching his twentieth birthday. By the time he had turned 22, he had been shot at by ships and enemy aircraft over the Norwegian coastline; shot down three German aircraft before being hit himself and attempted a daring emergency landing in the sea; and, as if that was not enough, saved the life of his navigator. He spent his twenty-third birthday on a POW camp in Germany. At that age, I had barely started a working career. Some difference!

It is fair to say that most allied pilots of Second World War were young, but Eriksrud seemed barely grown up. Photographs of him back then speak volumes—his face and eyes shine with child-like excitement, naivety, and bewilderment at living in a world turned on its head. But in those days, there simply was no time to spare: you grew up fast.

The idea of translating the book of a Norwegian pilot into English had already been with me for some time when I first started this project. My second reading of Eriksrud's memoirs was enough to convince me that his book was the perfect choice. It was old enough not to cause too much trouble with the original publisher, for one thing, who had disappeared decades ago and whose company had been broken and bought up several times since. Another important factor in my decision was the Eriksrud family itself. Eriksrud passed away in 2004, and even though his relatives might easily have been averse to the project, his son Sven trusted and helped me out in any way he could. He gave me essential information and photographs, and I am very grateful for his support and input. Thank you very much, Sven.

But as soon as I started work on the book, I encountered a stumbling block: Finn probably wrote in some haste, so didn't dwell much on either names, situations, or dates. On the few occasions that he does refer to friends and colleagues, he usually sticks to their first names, leaving no clue as to who these people were—in one case, he also misspells a friend's name. I therefore went through page after page taking note of names, places, ships, and towns Eriksrud mentions but does not explain, and later researched them, trying to put the pieces together. The result is here for you to read and enjoy. It was a pleasure to dig in and re-discover the intricate details of Eriksrud's journey all those years ago. What strikes me the most about his writing is his understatement of events, and dry sense of humour. More than often, he barely touches upon subjects which must have been both thrilling and petrifying. He gives himself no credit, instead recounting his exploits in an almost professional manner. However, read between the lines, and you will come to know a young man who was more often than not afraid and unsure of himself.

I would like to offer special thanks to fellow writers Chris Yeoman and Joseph Viney, who contributed a much needed grammar and spell check to the project. We have tried to stay true to the original text, perhaps sacrificing more advanced English expressions in favour of preserving Finn's literal meaning. As it should be.

Eriksrud dedicated his book to members of No. 333 Squadron who did not survive the war. I have taken the liberty of doing so here to three of his closest friends, who did not return: Gunnar Høverstad, Harold Odman, and Andreas Wyller. They were all true heroes, just like Finn Eriksrud.

Tor Idar Larsen

Eina, Norway,
January 2014.

Finn Eriksrud

Finn Eriksrud was born on 1 February 1922. His parents were Birger Eriksrud and Cathrine Harboe Eriksrud. Finn had two siblings, Emil and Rikke. According to Sven Eriksrud, Finn's son, they lived in a harmonious household with a steady income, even throughout the volatile 1930s. Birger was a lawyer in Oslo, and Finn grew up in Besserud, not far from the suburb of Holmenkollen. Like many Norwegians, he was an eager skier, but he also enjoyed sailing in the Oslofjord, where his family had a summer house on Gåsøya Island. He started school a year early, but did not seem to suffer much from the early start. He went to the Slemdal elementary school and then the Ris middle school. He graduated with an examen artium in the spring of 1940 and immediately took up law at the University of Oslo the following autumn. Shortly afterwards, he decided to escape occupied Norway and join the war effort. This is his story.

A young Finn Eriksrud at a photographer's in Oslo. (*Finn Eriksrud's collection*)

1

Escape from Norway

It was late evening in the autumn of 1940. The rain was pouring down so hard that Gunnar Høverstad and I had to struggle forward inch by inch by the east side of Lake Iddefjord. We were both unpleasantly soaked. We had walked for two hours without finding a single boat we could use to get across the fjord with. We hadn't really made any plans either, but simply hoped we could find one to get over the fjord and escape the occupation.

We had since early that season been thinking of escaping to Sweden, and from there on travelling to England. When the war came to Norway, neither Gunnar nor myself had participated in the fight, so we felt it was about time we did something. We had both graduated that year, and received the final grades we needed to go to university. In September, we were both accepted at the University of Oslo. Gunnar started language studies, and I law. Further studies never really happened that autumn. Too much going on around us for us to focus on learning. We kept hearing about friends we knew who had disappeared. We suspected they had gone to England, either over the North Sea or via Sweden.

One day that autumn I ran into Gunnar at university. We talked about this and that, and then Gunnar asked me, 'are you coming with me to England?'

I wasn't really surprised, because we had already discussed how best to escape, and how we could get to England as quickly as possible, and which route was the safest. Crossing the North Sea would obviously be the fastest way, but neither of us had any connections in western Norway. We didn't know who to contact in Oslo to get us in touch with the right people, either. However, Gunnar had heard a rumour that you only needed to get to Stockholm to be flown out straight to England. We therefore decided to walk across the border to Sweden. We didn't need much preparation for this journey, and the chances of us reaching our goal were about 100 to one.

After our conversation that day, we decided to leave the next afternoon. We would take the train to Halden, and then walk along Lake Iddefjord until we found a rowing boat we could borrow.

Everything had gone smoothly so far, and no one had asked us for any form of ID. Not on the train, and not in Halden either. Of course, we did not have the papers necessary for such travel. Still, we both had the feeling that everyone looked at us strangely when we got off the train at Halden. We were, after all, carrying two large backpacks with two large sleeping bags attached to them. Had people looked just a little closer, they would have seen how nervous we were as we left that station.

We had left the road quite early on, and began to walk along the shoreline. We didn't walk at a fast pace, either, as it was pitch black and we didn't dare use any torches. The mountainside came down all the way into the fjord, thus making it impossible for us to follow the shoreline, so we had to walk a long way around these obstacles. I thought we made a lot of noise, especially when we climbed over the hills and rocks, kicking stones into the water. The splash from those rocks as they hit the water seemed so loud that we were convinced they could be heard for miles and miles. However, after another 30 minutes of walking we finally found a boat tied to a little pier with the oars on board. Gunnar and I felt a little awkward about just taking the boat. We assumed that the owner was used to his boat disappearing on dark nights, but all the same, to ease our conscience, we left him 50 Nok and a message saying he would find his boat on the other side of the lake.

The rain had also stopped by now, and it was quickly replaced by a thick fog. We could barely see the lights on the other side of the fjord. We got on board the little rowing boat as quietly as we could, and started to row. We neither saw nor heard anyone on the way over, and we did reach the other, Swedish side. We were lucky, for there was a little hut close to where we came ashore. We got inside easily, and fell asleep for a few hours to regain our strength.

At first light, we set course for the Swedish town of Strømstad. It was a pretty long march. We met many Swedes, but no one spoke to us, and we reached the town without trouble around noon. We immediately started to ask around for the Norwegian legation, but before we got to find out where it was, we were stopped by a Swedish policeman and taken to the police station. We were then presented to an officer, who asked us what we had been up to, and why we had come to Sweden.

'Maybe you have done something wrong, since arriving here?' he enquired.

I was pretty green back then, even greener than I am now, so I thought the right answer was to tell him no. We had not done anything wrong. Gunnar wasn't much smarter, and added that we did not like Germans, and would like to travel to the Norwegian Embassy in Stockholm. We both thought that we would be sent back to Norway if we told the police we had committed any kind of criminal act. But the police officer smiled, and informed us that he regrettably had to send us back to Norway, since we had no reason to seek refuge in Sweden.

'But,' he said, 'if you come back some other time, at least make up a good story when you're asked why you have come here.'

We tried to protest, but to no prevail. Nothing we could say helped. We were fed and fell asleep in a cell, waiting for darkness to arrive. In the late afternoon, we were woken up and transferred to a waiting car which took us back to where we had come from, and back across the lake in a motor boat. As we disappeared into the woods, the Swedish official in charge of us went to the manned Norwegian border post to tell them to forget the entire affair.

So for us, the fun didn't last very long. Within 18 hours of escaping Norway, there we were once more, and with only a couple of hard lessons to show for it. No one knew we had even been to Sweden, though I think our families had a sneaky suspicion that ours was no regular trip.

We went back to university, and studied until Christmas of 1940. I strolled around campus pretending to read. I kept hearing about disappearances.

One day soon after Christmas, Gunnar and I were on a ski trip in Nordmarka when we met a friend of ours named Børne. We had not seen him from some time, and as we started chatting, he told us he had heard we had been across the border. He had plans to leave himself, and would like information on where it was safest to cross. Both Gunnar and I were initially surprised to learn that Børne actually knew we had been to Sweden. When we confronted him with this, he said he didn't really remember who told him.

Gunnar believed the best way to get to Sweden was by rail: to take the train to the border town of Magnor, disembark there, walk across the border, then get back on the train on the other side. Both Børne and I thought this plan a little too risky, for the area would be full of German soldiers. We were of the opinion that it was safest to cross the border on skis somewhere empty and out of the way. But Gunnar stuck to his guns: finally, he went his own way and we went ours. Gunnar took the train the next morning, and got to Sweden without difficulty. We later discovered that he arrived in Stockholm three days before us.

Børne and I began to make our way the day after Gunnar. It had been a sleepless night for me. I wondered what my future would hold. My mother had seen my backpack, fully packed and ready to go, in the closet. She knew what I was up to. She probably wasn't very pleased, but realised there was no way around my leaving. My father didn't seem to notice anything at all. That afternoon, my mother produced her priceless cookies, and begged me to eat as many of them as possible. Naturally, I did not have much of an appetite.

I was up early the next morning and skiied down the street. The clock had not yet struck seven, and it was still dark. I had taken this path to school every day for so many years, but that day I did it with a very special feeling. When would I be doing this again?

Børne and I took the first morning train to Kongsvinger, another border town. We didn't have any travel documents this time either, but things went surprisingly well. At Kongsvinger station we hitched a ride in a car that drove us some distance east. The rest of the way we did on skis. The snow was poor, but it didn't give us trouble. By nine in the afternoon, we had passed that long, empty line across the woods that separated Norway and Sweden.

We hadn't see another soul since leaving the car. After crossing over into Sweden, we sat down for a well-deserved rest. Then, we continued eastwards for about an hour. It was pitch black, but we spotted a single light in the forest and headed in its direction. A couple of Swedish workers were staying in a little hut, and we got to sleep in their beds that night.

The next morning, a border policeman came by and took us to Lekvatnet. The police officer from the Swedish town of Torsby arrived later that day, and we were interrogated in detail. I had a learned a few things since my last escape, and we had agreed on a story about how we were caught printing illegal newspapers, and how we barely managed to get away. This was accepted, and the police officer drove us down to Torsby in his car, where he delivered us to a colleague called Larsen. We had to wait a few days before the authorities approved for travel in Sweden. Larsen was a very nice man indeed. He told us he often had visitors like us. In the afternoon he brought us to see a film at the local cinema. My impression was that he did it because he was proud to present his 'prisoners' to the townspeople.

Børne had been clever and brought his passport, and it was this that allowed us to exchange a few hundred Nok for Swedish currency. The day after, which was a Sunday, we bought tickets for the train to Stockholm, and arrived there safely at night.

2

Stuck in Stockholm

The Norwegian legation in Stockholm wasn't open that night, so we had to find a hotel. On Monday morning we reported to the legation, happy and pleased with our progress. We were led from one office to the next for questioning, and finally our identities were confirmed. We told them what we had heard in Oslo—that we would be sent to England immediately, and that it was only a matter of getting all our paperwork in order. It was then that our first disappointment dawned on us: we had no military education. The only experience we had to offer was this 72-hour voluntary mission, obviously nothing to speak of. The only thing the Norwegian legation could do for us was sign us onto the long list of people in this same predicament. For the time being, all we could do was stay in Stockholm and wait. Many others ahead of us on this list had already been stuck in Stockholm for several months, unable to travel further.

The Norwegian legation in Stockholm

The Norwegian legation in Stockholm had its roots in the dissolution of Swedo-Norwegian union in 1905. It was part of the free Norwegian state administration. At the outbreak of the Second World War, the legation had four employees; by the end of the war, a total of 1,200 people worked there.

The legation played a vital role in the war effort, chiefly through its coordination of Norwegian refugees. A military office was established in 1941, and this was later split into two separate headquarters: one for intelligence, the XU, and one for Norway's military resistance group, Milorg. When Finn and Gunnar came to Stockholm, Jens Bull was in charge of the legation. Fifty thousand Norwegian refugees found their way to Sweden during the war.

Thankfully, a place to stay was rapidly arranged for us. I was sent to a guest house, while Børne had family to stay with. We got two food tickets each day, which gave us access to two delicious meals if we wished. We also received a weekly allowance of 5 Nok.

The next day I met Gunnar again. He wished me a warm welcome to Stockholm, and told me how easy it had been for him to cross the border. He had been told the same as me at the legation, and we discussed eagerly what we should do to do move on as soon as possible. We returned to the legation once more, and talked to secretary Wendelbo. He told us that nothing could be done, given the circumstances. However, if we managed to come up with the travel money ourselves, he could help us get hold of the necessary visas. It was a lot of money we had to get hold of, about 3,000 Nok. Neither Gunnar nor I had family in Sweden or America to lend us this sum. Our only option was to get in touch with our parents back in Norway and ask them to send it to us. By chance, a courier was leaving for Norway that day, and we managed to send a message with him.

We had nothing more to do than meander around Stockholm until an answer came from Norway. After fourteen days of waiting impatiently, Wendelbo told us that the money had arrived safely. We went to the legation once more, and quite right too, for the money was there for both Gunnar and me. A telegram was then sent to London to get us permits to stay in Canada, the answer to which could take up to three to four weeks. Yet again, our biggest problem was how to pass the time. We went out on skis a fair bit. Personally, I was very happy, and acted as a ski instructor in one of the parks in Stockholm. I taught many young children. In the evenings, Gunnar and I played a lot of bridge or went to the cinema.

After a month, another visit to the legation told us no answer from London had arrived yet. Our morale suffered a blow; our situation seemed bleak. Still, we had a better luck than those among us without money at their disposal. Some of them were terribly depressed, and tried to get out of Stockholm by any means possible. Some Norwegians even went to the Chinese Embassy to volunteer for the war against Japan, only to be told that China had no use for them. So they carried on to the Greek Embassy, and asked to be sent to Greece, and got the same answer there—no use for such men.

Gunnar and I got visas for Canada in early March. At last, we were getting somewhere. Our plan was first to travel over Siberia to Vladivostok, then to Japan, and from there to the west coast of America. However, the Japanese legation was in the habit of rejecting most applications for travel permits, so we looked for an alternative route. The best way forward we came up with was to go to Moscow, then Odessa, and then Istanbul by boat. From Istanbul we would get on the Baghdad–Basra railway line, and then from Basra boat to Bombay. We had money enough to get this far. Once in Bombay, all we could do would be to hope for passage on a boat bound for England or Canada. After our Canadian visas were out of the way, we would have to secure Indian, Syrian, Turkish, and finally Russian visas too. This required persuading each legation that we were not going to their country to stay, but simply passing through. At the end of March 1941, all the visas seemed to be in order: we could walk down to Cook's travel agency in Stockholm and order our tickets like ordinary tourists. We got tickets for a flight out of Stockholm on the 4th of April, almost a whole year since Norway had entered the war on the side of the Allies. We asked ourselves, would we ever get to contribute before the whole thing was over?

3

Dodgy Bars and Friendly Swedes

On the morning of April 4th, Gunnar and I met at the bus station for a short drive out to Bromma Airfield. At the airport, our passports were stamped, and our baggage thoroughly checked and weighed. This was my first time in an aircraft. I was more than excited and pretty tense about it, wondering how I would handle it mentally. I had been thinking of becoming a pilot myself, hopefully before the war was over. I handled the trip well, as I had predicted. We flew high over the clouds, and could only catch the occasional glimpse of the Baltic Sea beneath us. Spring had definitely arrived down there, and I observed large flakes of ice floating in the blue water. They looked like pathways across the sea.

Bromma Airfield

Bromma Airfield was opened in Stockholm in 1936 by King Gustav V, and was one of the very first European airfields to have paved runways from the start of construction. Swedish and British aircraft operated from this airfield during the war. Flights to Britain often carried Norwegian and Danish refugees, so the rumour Eriksrud heard in Oslo had some truth to it. This service mostly only applied to important personnel or refugees with specialist skills, or the transfer of important documents and equipment. The route between Britain and Sweden was also dangerous, and several aircraft were lost to the Germans, for instance two neutral Swedish DC-3s. Finn Eriksrud and Gunnar Høverstad were simply two students with a strong desire to do their bit—hardly priority passengers. The airfield was also a natural hot-spot for German spies.

We made a quick stop at a Russian airport, where our baggage was again scrupulously examined. We were then, quite literally, searched from head to toe, and the Swiss army-knife I had on me was found, packed in a large box, and sealed up in all seriousness. I was given strict orders not to open the box under any circumstance until I had left Russian borders. When we finally arrived back at the aircraft, they had even removed all our newspapers.

Apparently, it was forbidden to bring foreign press into the country. We went to our seats once more, and continued onwards to Moscow, arriving there in the late afternoon.

The journey from Stockholm had taken us about four to five hours. We were four Norwegians travelling from Stockholm that morning. Besides myself and Gunnar were two officers from the Norwegian Army Air Force. At the airport in Moscow we were met by a representative from the Russian travel agency Intourist and brought to the Savoy Hotel. There we met ten other Norwegians, who had come from Stockholm via Finland. We were to depart together for Odessa that very afternoon, so I didn't get a chance to do the sights in Moscow. The only impression I did form of the Russian capital and its three million inhabitants was that it had prodigiously wide streets. This city's trams also seemed to have more people on the outside than on the inside.

We were given a lunch pack for the train journey—bread, butter, and a few eggs—for there would be no opportunity to purchase anything on board. However, tea was served throughout the journey by an old woman. She made it on a primitive stove in the train's small hallway. You could easily convert the compartment into a sleeping-carriage, which we did, though we didn't get much sleep on account of the driver, who seemed to think he was controlling a cargo, not a passenger train. Every time the train stopped, one of us would be thrown out of bed and onto the floor. The same thing happened whenever the train started up again. After a while, however, we got the hang of it and instinctively managed to hold on tight in our sleep.

The landscape outside was flat and dull. There were some forests between the large fields, but nothing else. We never spoke with the Russians, since none of us knew the Russian language. We had no idea what they were saying, and they had no clue what we were saying, even though we tried speaking in German, English, and French to them. After 48 hours on the train to Odessa, we finally arrived. We were greeted by another representative of Intourist, who took us to our hotel. This was situated close to the Black Sea, with a beautiful view of the harbour and the water, but didn't feel especially different to European hotels. But visitors knew without a doubt that they were in Russia, because of the indescribable smell. It hit us right in the face wherever we went in this huge, strange country. What this smell really was I have no idea, but I have heard many speaking of this 'Russian smell'.

We discovered that it was not in our interest to convert our dollars into Russian currency, since the exchange rate was not in our favour. A couple of fellow travellers had come up with a smart strategy: they brought a few suits along with them and sold them in the city for a tidy sum of roubles. Because we would only stay in Odessa for one day, we had problems using up all the roubles from the sale. All the Russian money in our possession had to be used up before we left Russia. The only thing left to do was to purchase copious amounts of vodka, champagne, and Cossack shirts.

Gunnar was a big fan of opera. He had heard all the operas in Stockholm, and quickly ascertained that there was a large opera theatre in Odessa. He eagerly dragged me there with him, and I do not regret going at all. I didn't understand much of what was going on in front of me, but it was very interesting to sit in this large building and observe all the different people who had come to watch the show. My impression was that all of them just came as they were, straight from work. They seemed to appreciate the singing and the music, their pleasure in it was obvious.

The next day we were taken on a sightseeing tour of Odessa. The city was probably very pretty, once. The parks were large and the streets wide here as well. But the buildings all needed a fresh coat of paint and general restoration work. The place looked and felt like a coastal city.

Our boat to Istanbul that day was delayed, and there was a rumour going around that it wouldn't depart at all. We knew we were in deep trouble if this was true. Thankfully, this proved not to be the case, and the next afternoon we packed our suitcases once more, only to have them searched again. I wanted to bring a rouble with me as a souvenir, and had kept it hidden in the fold of one of my trouser legs, but the border guard found it immediately. Instead of smuggling it out of the country, I bought cookies with it so I could finally be on my way. The boat was Russian, and very comfortable. This pleased enormously, because I had caught a bad cold, and spent most of my time aboard tied to my bed.

When it dawned on us that the boat would stop by Varna in Bulgaria, a city occupied by German troops, a chill ran down our spines. We were further alarmed when the boat came to a halt by the harbour and we saw German soldiers on patrol. Someone told us that we had to be careful about showing our faces on deck. The Germans could reportedly photograph us, and send the photos back to Norway. Back then, this seemed more than likely, though I suspect this was pure conjecture. We were more than pleased the next day when we discovered the boat was out on the open sea once again. One afternoon, we sailed through Bosporus, or the highway of Constantinople, as it was called. We stood at the bow with Asia Minor on one side, and Europe on the other.

The pass is 30 km long, and its smallest strait just 500 m wide. It's very shallow indeed, in some places no more than 20 m deep. All the rivers running out into the Black Sea mean that the current is nearly always running outwards.

On the oriental banks, we saw ruins of fortresses which had stood there for more than two thousand years. Apparently, these were the vestiges of Alexander the Great's passage through here on his conquests all the way to

Indus. For the first time in my life, I really felt that there was a sort of reality to all this ancient history I was taught in school. It had all been so distant and alien when I studied it.

Sailing into Istanbul is quite the experience. Steep hills rise out of the sea all around you. They stretch to 250 m. I saw a long chain of connected villages, castles, and fortresses. Everything was green and luscious. From time to time, the minarets of mosques protruded in their singular fashion.

The visit to customs in Istanbul was effortless. When that was over and done with, we drove to our hotel in a taxi. On the ride I tried to find out whether there was any traffic rules at all in this city—it didn't look like it one bit. If our driver couldn't overtake a tram on one side, he simply tried on the other. Car horns went nonstop—it was near impossible to distinguish our horn from anyone else's, so unanimously did they sound. I was very happy to get to our hotel still in one piece.

When we sat down to dinner, a Turkish man entered the room and introduced himself as our guide. We thought he would show us all the cultural sights of the city, but we were wide of the mark. He brought us straight to a cabaret, and introduced us to the hostess of the establishment. We came into an ill-lit room with a few tables places by the walls and a modest dance-floor in the centre. Five men were seated on a small stage, playing their music. The venue itself looked pretty boring. The audience appeared to be a mix of foreigners we could not place, and we only managed to separate Turks from the rest by their slightly darker skin tone, as they were dressed as Europeans. There was nothing special about the band either, they simply played the normal jazz music you heard everywhere. We had not been there for long before a few young women asked if we wanted to dance. We did not have anything against the idea at all, but when we had finished they sat down with us without invitation and said they wanted champagne. We were perfect gentlemen, and ordered what they asked for. I think a simple soda factory could have produced more convincing champagne than the stuff we were served. Yet it seemed the women liked the taste, and wanted more. It wasn't cheap either. These ladies were small and thin, but covered in either make up or powder. There were no language barriers, as this time we fared well in German and French. Nothing odd about that though, for very few of them were Turks.

We were beginning to get a bit tired of all this champagne ordering, when two Swedes came over to our table. They had gathered from our appearance that we were Norwegians, and were engineers working in Istanbul. They sat down beside us and began a conversation which ended in an invitation to their home. We thanked the ladies for their time and the champagne we drank, and left. We spent the rest of the evening with the Swedes. They told us about Turkey—they had been there for last five years—and we told them about the latest events in Stockholm.

Our Swedish hosts had a little, typically European apartment. They were most interested to hear about life back at home. They had followed the war in the papers with interest, and firmly supported Norway's cause. They were most keen to hear about whether or not Sweden would enter the war, in which case they would risk being stuck in Istanbul. They had often spoken about going home before it was too late.

The day after our friendly encounter with the Swedes, we got hold of a real guide who took us to the bazars. They consisted of a myriad of narrow little streets, criss-crossing all over the place. There were stands everywhere selling the most fascinating things, especially carpets. It all gave me the feeling of being underground, where not a single ray of sunshine was let through. Gunnar and I decided to keep close to the guide. It was obvious that you could get lost very fast in such a place. Finally, a taste of that special oriental mystique that I always had been keen on getting to know better. Packed with people and an endless chatter, we couldn't make head or tail of it. Some Norwegians bought souvenir they hoped to bring back home one day. They paid the asking price, but this was not normal practice in countries such as this, and I am sure they were more than cheated. Later on, we had plenty of fun watching the endless negotiations of customers and salesmen. It was obvious that the seller asked much more than what the product was worth, an attitude that had endured the ages yet always appeared new.

Around the world: an unidentified ship gives us a glimpse into Eriksrud's travels in 1941. (*Finn Eriksrud's collection*)

From the bazars we went to look at Sultan Achmed's mosque. It was a truly monumental piece of construction. We had the feeling that the place was more of a tourist attraction than a place of worship. To get inside, we had to take off our shoes and socks and put slippers on. The floors in all the rooms were draped with inch-thick carpets.

We had no time to see anything else in Istanbul, for the next day we were off again.

4

Revolt in Baghdad

We were transported over to Skutari on the other side of the Bosporus, and from there would take the railway line to Baghdad. This turned to be a comfortable trip. We travelled in modern carriages, and the landscape was very different from what we had got used to back in Russia. The railway line first went by the Sea of Marmara a short while, and then we went into the mountains. We felt more at home here, with the forests, mountains, and valleys. From time to time, the train would enter a tunnel.

We stopped by Ankara, but only for about half an hour, so we did not venture outside the station area. After that short stop, the railway line headed south again. We were closing in on Syria. The landscape outside started to become more desert-like. We passed the border into Syria a few hours later, and a few hours after that reached Aleppo, an important railway connection point. The line then turned north, somewhere in Syria. On the first day of Easter, we reached Mosul in Iraq, famous for its oil. From here, the line followed the River Tigris to Baghdad.

As far as the eye could see, there was only sand. It was mind boggling to even think that this country was once called Mesopotamia, and was the cradle of a great and advanced culture.

On the second day of Easter (14 April 1941), we reached Baghdad. We were greeted at the train station by representatives from several hotels in the city. They started to discuss certain matters with us, but when they realised we didn't understand a word of what they said, they shifted their focus and started to argue among themselves instead. The whole matter was apparently about which hotel we should stay at, and which hotel was the best. The whole thing ended with our suitcases being put on a horse-drawn cab. We had no choice but to follow. We finally ended up at Hotel Semiramis. There were already twelve Norwegians living there. It was a very fancy hotel, close to the Tigris. The water in the river was terribly black and extremely muddy. We never went for the swim we had planned.

We spent a whole week in Baghdad. The plan was for us to travel further by aircraft, but the flight was cancelled for some reason. We had to wait for tickets for a boat to Bombay instead. It started to get really hot in Baghdad, and the European clothes we had did not suit the climate one bit. On our very first day in Baghdad, Gunnar and I went out to buy more fitting outfits. I got hold of a tropical helmet, short pants, and a new shirt. If we hadn't looked like tourists when we arrived, we certainly did now. We strolled around the city on our own, looking at anything of interest. One day we dared to venture down to the narrow streets near the river. It was horribly dirty down there, very ugly, and the streets were narrow and difficult to manoeuvre in. We frequently passed Arabs with wide open cuts and injuries, or with a missing arm or leg. We had reached quite far into this strange, dirty world when a rock suddenly flew past us at terrific speed. We turned instantly, but didn't spot anything out of the ordinary. Seconds later, another rock came flying past us. We decided it was time to get out of there. The Arabs most have taken us for Englishmen, who were not very popular in Iraq at the time. Fourteen days later, a riot actually broke out, but by then we were already in Bombay.

Those Norwegians who came to Baghdad after us ended up in the middle of that mess. I was later told they had been in Basra when the riot broke out, and because the Arabs refused to work in the harbour, the Norwegians had to do the work themselves in order to leave the country. They did this as the airport close by was being bombed! The fact that they were working with boxes of ammunition, and had to transfer it to the ship, far from alleviated the situation.

Gunnar and I also went to the cinema one evening in Baghdad. As Europeans we were shown to the best seats in the theatre, which was high up and far back. We would have liked to have sat closer to the screen, but were denied this request. I got the impression that very few in the audience were even faintly interested in the film. Most of them seemed to have bought a ticket so they could take a nap.

There was one thing that had worried us considerably since we came to Baghdad. Wherever we went, three tall and dark skinned Arabs kept following us. They also stayed at the same hotel as us, went to the same films, and came to the nightclub we visited one night. They were on our tail once we left the nightclub, too. There were no horse-drawn cabs to catch, so we had to walk. This was far from pleasant. It was far to walk as well, and plenty of Arabs were patrolling the streets with guns at their shoulders. We were left alone though, and reached the hotel safely. We had no idea what these guys wanted to do with us. They never spoke to us, but we always felt their presence close by. There was something truly mysterious and oriental about those three men. They wore long black capes, with white headwear flapping in the wind. This wasn't exactly as we had envisioned the relatives of Harun-al-Rasjid and the city of the *One Thousand and One Nights*.

It didn't feel like there was much left of Baghdad's period of greatness. Only a few towers and mosques from those days still stood. We had by now been walking around and looking at this city for a week's time, and of course, it was interesting enough. But, this wasn't why we escaped Norway and German occupation. We wanted to get going.

Finally, a ship carrying troops arrived in Basra. This was going back to Bombay, so we asked if we could kindly get a ride. We could. A small train took us to Basra, where we boarded ship. It was a very interesting trip down Shatt al-Arab, for the river was so named after Euphrates and Tigris, which merged together there. The land was green and luscious as far as the eye could see, with many canals and small rivers in all directions. I got no pleasure from this ride on account of the appalling heat and an inexplicably bad fever. One evening, Gunnar found me in a corridor with just a sheet wrapped around my waist. He helped me back to my bed. I remember nothing whatsoever of this bizarre incident.

Revolt in Baghdad

What Finn may be referring to is the pro-Nazi Iraqi military coup which began on 1 April 1941, in an attempt to overthrow the pro-British regime of 'Abd al-Illah. The coup aimed at full Iraqi independence from the British, as opposed to the limited freedoms granted by the Independence Treaty of 1932. The Iraqi insurgents turned to German intelligence and accepted German military assistance to this end. The ensuing change of government led to a British invasion and subsequent occupation of Iraq until 1947. If Eriksrud's stated date of arrival—14 April 1941—is correct, the British will have launched their campaign only four days later, landing forces in Basra on the 18th.

Finn also refers to other Norwegians in trouble in Basra two weeks after their departure. In effect, the fighting continued until 2 May 1941, though this was mostly confined to Habbinya and Fallujah. The pro-Nazi Iraqi forces were driven back to Baghdad, which fell within a week. This cleared the way for the restoration of the pro-British regency.

After a couple of days we arrived in Karachi, west of the Indus delta by the Arabian Sea. We formed our first impressions of an Indian city here. The buildings looked modern, but were poorly maintained. House pets walked freely in the streets, and mothers washed their children in the gutter. We saw more of this in Bombay, which we travelled to the same afternoon. This is where our tickets expired. The rest of our journey was up to destiny now.

We got rooms at the Hotel Majestic, and the next day went straight to the Norwegian consul to ask him for help to travel further. He told us that, for the moment, there were no Norwegian ships in the harbour, but he would do everything he could to get us on our way. Only four days later, fourteen Norwegian officers left with the Wilhelmsen ship *Tayyang*. A couple of days later, six more officers left for Calcutta and from there boarded a ship to America. When we had left Stockholm, there had been only four of us Norwegians. But more and more had attached themselves to our party in the course of our travels, so by the time we reached Bombay there were about hundred and fifty of us, all with the desire to report for military duty in England or Canada. Obviously, not everyone could stay in hotels, so we moved to a camp outside the city. We ended up having to stay in Bombay for fourteen days. It was terribly warm outside. We used to enjoy spending the mornings by a little saltwater swimming pool just outside the city. The water was changed every time the tide came in. In the evenings, we usually went to the cinema. They were air-conditioned in Bombay, and felt very soothing, shut off from the pressing heat outside. You could really take a breather in there. I believe that it was only the wealthy Indians who went to the cinema. There were many pretty and charming Indian women around. They had long silk dresses, and literally dragged them along as they walked.

This was also our only chance to observe the Indians' quite unusual caste system. In reality, it digs deep into the way of life in India. This system is one of the major reasons why uniting them under one nation is so problematic. There are in fact over two thousand different casts, and it is impossible to go from one caste to another.

One day we were out with the consul's wife on a sightseeing trip. Among many things, she showed us the Malabar Hill. Lots of predators flew over this area. Whenever they saw fit, they would dive straight down and catch a leg or an arm, which they ate. After they were done with their free meal, they would drop the bone somewhere in the city.

We also had the honour of visiting an Indian family. They lived in a big, modern complex close to the sea. Part of their estate had a large swimming pool, but otherwise their house was decorated much like what we were used to back home, though instead of radiators they had big fans attached to the ceiling. These always circulated, so the air was always in motion.

We also insisted on getting a 100-per-cent Indian meal. We later regretted it, because we really struggled eating the stuff. It was a mixture of rice and small pieces of meat and a terrible type of curry. The son in the household was engaged to a Norwegian girl, but he hadn't heard anything from her since the outbreak of war. He enthusiastically asked us whether we perhaps knew the girl, since we all came from Norway. We obviously didn't. He had met this young girl on a trip there, somewhere up in the mountains. I don't remember where exactly. All he wished for was a short war, so he could go back and marry her.

We wanted to ask his two sisters to the films the same evening, so we asked him how best to proceed. It was far from as easy as back in Norway. We were welcome to ask them, but had to bring him and the rest of the family along with us. Nothing came of it either way, as we left Bombay before we had managed to invite every family member.

Walking the streets of Bombay was a bother due to large flocks of filthy children who followed you wherever you went asking for money. And if it wasn't children, it was the cab drivers, coming up on our side and making it quite impossible not to take their cab somewhere. We also felt much pity for a small boy who asked to polish our shoes. We let him do it. We shouldn't have let him though, because about twenty or thirty children quickly showed up and offered the same service. We had to run away from them, they were that many.

Life jacket on, ready to jump ship! This might perhaps have been taken during a drill aboard the *Warwick Castle*. (*Finn Eriksrud's collection*)

5

The Atlantic Crossing

We had been in Bombay for exactly fourteen days, and were beginning to get very bored with life in general. We were simply very impatient to get on with it. That same day, we were finally told by the consul that we had been given permission to travel onwards to England aboard the troop ship *Warwick Castle*. The ship was due to sail around the Cape of Good Hope the next day. It was massive, weighing in at over 20,000 tonnes.

MV Warwick Castle

MV *Warwick Castle* was a British troop transport ship weighing 20,107 tonnes, and was one of the largest sunk during the war. It was completed in 1930 in Belfast and owned by the Union-Castle Mail SS Company, London. It was requisitioned by the Admiralty as a troopship in September 1939, and sank just a few months after Finn Eriksrud travelled from Gibraltar to Glasgow aboard it. It met its demise on 14 November 1942, at the hands of U-413, commanded by Gustav Poel, about 200 miles north-west of Cape Espichel, Portugal. The ship sank an hour after it was hit by torpedoes. Sixty-one crew members and thirty-four service personnel perished, though 366 souls were saved. Among the casualties was Capt. Henry Leepman-Shaw, who died on the rescue ship aged 57 and was posthumously awarded a Mention in Despatches on 18 May 1943 for services rendered during Operation Torch, the Allied landings in North Africa in November 1942.

We were travelling as regular privates, and two men were given one cabin to share. The heat still bothered us immensely, so we kept our faces glued to the ventilation system in the cabins at all times. It was too hot to eat anything, so we drank plenty of tea instead. We sweated that stuff out again in no time. We spent most of our time on board reading and talking to other Norwegians. Many of them had tragic stories to tell from their time with the Norwegian Army during the invasion in 1940.

Every passenger on board with their life jackets firmly on. (*Finn Eriksrud's collection*)

Warwick Castle. (Tor Idar Larsen's collection)

The daily routines onboard the ship were broken once we passed the equator. The captain dressed up as Neptune, and in all seriousness baptised anyone who had not previously passed the Equator. We also celebrated Norway's national day aboard this ship, on the 17th of May. The captain invited us all into the big first-class dining room for dinner.

After six days' journey we reached Durban. We could not get a spot by the pier, and stayed in the harbour for two days waiting for our turn. When we finally arrived on shore we were, to our surprise, greeted by several Norwegians who lived there. They took us for a ride in a car further inland. We most enjoyed seeing wild monkeys and a camp for Italian POWs. These soldiers had been taken prisoner during the North African campaign, and transported to Durban in the ship called *Bergensfjord*. We saw that ship down at the harbour, it was grey and ugly.

SS Bergensfjord

SS *Bergensfjord* was a Norwegian troop transport ship during the Second World War. It was built in Birkenhead, England, in 1913. Its first journey took it from Bergen, Norway, to New York in September that year. It served as a troop transport ship for the duration of the war, and went back into regular service after hostilities ended. It was scrapped in 1959.

We spent the afternoon in a Norwegian home, where we got an excellent meal of real Norwegian sandwiches. Unfortunately for us, we had to go aboard again quite early. When Gunnar and I got back down to the harbour, we were met by a sight that had drawn many people's attention: two Norwegian boys driving a rickshaw at full speed, with the rickshaw chap nicely seated in the back.

The next day, it was our intention to meet the Norwegian family again, and we very much looking forward to it. However, the ship left at seven in the morning, much to our disappointment. We were now sailing along South Africa's coastline, and finally rounded the Cape. We saw Table Mountain, which was just like it was portrayed in our geography books back home. A few hours later we arrived in Cape Town. We had excitedly anticipated going all the way up to Table Mountain, but the weather had deteriorated such that the whole mountain was draped in fog and rain, so there was no point in going up there.

The Norwegians in Durban had found out that we had little money, and we were wired one pound each from our friends when we came ashore in Cape Town. We were extremely happy, and it was such a nice gesture.

The ship *Tayyang* had already arrived in Cape Town, having left Bombay some time before us. On board the *Tayyang* was a Norwegian officer bound for England, though the ship was travelling further on to Canada. He asked if I wanted to trade places with him. It was better for me to actually get to Canada, so I had nothing against switching. The only problem was that I had to say goodbye to Gunnar and the other chaps I had become friendly with. However, we were sure we would meet again quite soon anyway. The next morning, I left Cape Town aboard the *Tayyang*.

The Tai Yang

Eriksrud got the name slightly wrong when he wrote in 1945. The ship's name was *The Tai Yang*, indeed a Wilhelmsen Line ship, in service between 1929 and 1962. Ironically, it was built in Kiel, Germany, by Deutsche Werke A.G. It left Cape Town on 1 June 1942, bound for Montreal. It arrived in Canada on 14 July with Eriksrud on board, after he traded places with a Norwegian officer. *The Tai Yang* usually sailed independently, rarely joining any convoys. The ship survived the war, and in 1962 was sold to Mousse Shipping Co., Cyprus. It was scrapped in Shanghai in 1970.

My switch meant that my next stop would be Montreal in Canada. We were in for some terrible weather on the first two days out to sea, and I decided not to eat anything. What I ate for breakfast that first morning, I got no use of anyway, if you know what I mean. However, we slowly came closer to the trade winds, and the weather improved for the better. On board were thirteen officers belonging to the Norwegian Army Air Force. I decided to seize the opportunity at hand and ask about the tests I would have to go through to become a pilot. To their entertainment and wild joy, I did exactly as they told me and stood on one leg with my eyes closed, my tongue out, and my arms outstretched for as long as I could. After practising these silly exercises for a good while, I managed to stand like this for five minutes. I was told that this was one of the most important tests I had to go through, but of course I later realised that they had just been making fun of me.

Each of us had to spend a few hours a day high up on the look-out for U-boats and German ships. There was plenty of German activity in these waters, and we had to zigzag to confound the enemy. During the night, however, we pushed straight on.

One day, just after breakfast, a series of sharp sounds came from the steam whistle. The captain had told us in advance that this would mean we had to get into the lifeboats as quickly as possible, and the entire ship erupted into complete chaos. We put on our life jackets, and got into the lifeboats hanging by the sides of the ship. Once we were on board and waiting for the next move, the captain came out smiling. It had just been a drill.

On another day, we saw a merchant vessel on the horizon. In the beginning we hardly took notice, but when it came closer we saw that it was coming straight towards us. The telegraphist tried to get in touch with the ship, but he got no response. We changed our course a few degrees further north, but the unknown ship followed by changing its direction as well. The *Tayyang* then changed its course northwards, but to no avail, as the other ship did the same. We became certain that the ship was a German commerce-raiding ship, coming to sink us. In the end we turned 180 degrees, and put both our engines on full speed. The telegraphist started to send out SOS signals. I already saw myself aboard this unknown ship, the Germans' captive. What would happen once I arrived in Germany, I dared not to think about at all. Our pursuer was only a few hundred metres away when it suddenly changed its course. I'm holding back when I say we were pleased when we saw the ship disappear in the distance. Later on, our captain was informed that it had been an American cargo ship. He used strong language when he voiced his opinion of the captain of the other ship. I was told allied vessels had orders to steer away from each other when they met on the open sea.

The general atmosphere on the ship after such an incident was tense. It didn't help when we got the news that an English ship was torpedoed nearby. One of our engines cut out at the same time, which didn't help either. For the rest of the trip we used either the starboard or the port engine, as one of them kept cutting out. Going at no more than 6 to 7 knots, we were a nice, fat target for anything hostile. The only weapon we had on board was a Krag-Jørgensen. The mood improved greatly when we got the news on the 23rd of June that Russia had entered the war on our side.

The rest of the voyage went quietly, except from when we entered the fog outside of Labrador, whereupon the whistle went constantly. On the 27th of June, we saw land. It was Novia Scotia. It didn't take long until we were in the St. Lawrence River. A wonderful view of Quebec followed, with its impressive fortress. Then onwards to Montreal.

The next day we arrived in Montreal, and the day after I took the train up to Toronto to report for duty at Little Norway. I already knew at the station in Montreal that I was on the right course, as I saw a Norwegian pilot walk past me with a Canadian girlfriend. She had written 'Little Norway' all over the back of her dress. I arrived in Toronto in the late afternoon. It had taken me five and a half months of travelling to reach my final destination. This was the first milestone of many to come.

6

Little Norway

When I arrived in Toronto in 1941, it had a population of 700,000. Outside Toronto are several islands where city-dwellers have their summer houses. Norway had situated its Air Force recruiting school in some old barracks on the west side of one of these islands, Centre Island, during the summer months of '41. The airfield was also situated at Centre Island, and called 'Island Airport'. The Norwegian Air Force also took it over. From there you could take a small ferry over the small channel to Toronto. This is where Little Norway was located.

Little Norway

After the south of Norway was surrendered to the invading German forces, Bjarne Øen, the temporary commander of the Norwegian Air Force, was tasked by Gen. Otto Ruge to travel to England and bring back aircraft for the ongoing struggle in the North. Part of his mission was also to investigate the possibilities of establishing a training base for Norwegian pilots in England or France. But Germany's advances both in Norway and on the European continent put a stop to this plan, and all eyes turned towards Canada instead. The Canadian government eagerly welcomed the Norwegians, and a deal was soon struck: both the Norwegian Navy and Army Air Force would establish themselves in Toronto, and join the RAF as Norwegian units, much like the Poles had done (the Navy Air Force would join the RAF Coastal Command). The training camp was quickly named Little Norway: it was Norwegian-built, just inside of Toronto's harbour area. Originally, the camp had room for about 700 men, and included the necessary utilities such as messes, a hospital, and offices. It was officially opened in November of 1940, but had already been operational for some months.

The first personnel arrived from England in the late summer of 1940. Many of these were pilots educated at Kjeller before the war and had escaped Norway aboard HMS *Devonshire* with King Haakon VII. They later expressed their bitterness towards their government for leaving England when it needed pilots the most during the Battle of Britain. Because of this decision, no Norwegian pilots got to participate in the Battle of Britain, even when some were in London at the time. Norwegian military leaders argued that they did not want the backbone of their Air Force to be 'lost' in English squadrons or killed in action. Yet pre-war educated pilots were still later to serve as the foundation of Norway's first squadrons in Britain. Official reluctance to offer pilots to the RAF during the Battle of Britain was perhaps the first of many disagreements between the government in exile and the Norwegian pilots on the ground in the Second World War. It was a common saying among pilots and ground crew that they were fighting for the king, and not for the government. Hostile feelings sometimes led to odd situations. A drunken Ottar Malm, one of the veterans of No. 331 Squadron, decided during a spell in London to take a taxi to Kingston House, the offices of the exiled administration. He got out of the taxi and urinated on one of the walls of the building, then returned to his friends.

Throughout the autumn of 1940, Norwegians arrived in Canada in increasingly high numbers. Danes and Swedes also joined them at Little Norway, Kaj Birksted and Kjeld Rønhøf perhaps the best known among them.

In the late spring of 1941, another camp was bought for use by Air Force personnel as both a recreational and educational camp. They named this camp 'Vesle Skaugum', after the king's countryside house in Norway. It was situated on a small strip of land between Dotty Lake and Oxbow Lake, about 200 km from Toronto.

In June 1941, a Northrop N-3PB collided with the ferry operating between Centre Island and Toronto. Instructor Finn S. Kjos and pupil Tron Harsvik did not see the ferry coming towards them in the foggy conditions. The aircraft touched the ferry and crashed into the lake. Both men aboard the Northrop were killed. This was perhaps the most serious accident at Little Norway, though far from the only one. Canadian officials started ruffling their feathers about all the hazardous flying, while newspapers speculated about when—not if—a Norwegian aircraft would crash in Toronto itself. The Norwegians had to make some quick decisions as to what to do next, and temporarily moved further flying instruction north of Toronto, to Emsdale. The airfield had no living quarters, and the pupils stayed in tents on the airfield.

In January 1943, another base was established at Muskoka, by Gravenhurst in Ontario. After the pupils had finished their initial training there, they were usually sent to either Moose Jaw or Medicine Hat for more advanced instruction under British command. Fighter pilots went to Moose Jaw and bomber pilots to Medicine Hat. Norwegians did well in sports, which was one thing, but more importantly, they also did very well indeed in their classes. Spitfire aces Svein Heglund and Martin Gran, for instance, finished first and second in their class at Moose Jaw, followed by glittering careers in the next couple of years.

Another view of Island Airport and Little Norway, Toronto: snow on the ground, and a low cloudbase. (*Finn Eriksrud's collection*)

When I arrived there in the summer of 1941, most barracks in Little Norway were already finished and put up. They were smartly laid out around a big lawn where we had drill commands twice a day. Eight o' clock in the morning, and one o' clock in the afternoon. In the autumn of 1941, while I was still there, the two nicest buildings of them all were constructed. One of them was Radio City, as they called it. It consisted of two floors, and was mostly used for sleeping quarters. Lectures were also held on the first floor. The other and most popular building of the two was the gymnastics hall, which included a sauna. It also had study rooms on the second floor. The barracks were well constructed, and were perhaps much too nice to be called barracks. They had central heating, and several layers of panel in the walls. They were also well equipped, with showers and washbasins. Our beds were stacked in twos on top of each other. Little Norway also had three kitchens: one for the privates, one for the sergeants, and one for the officers. The food from all three kitchens always came in decent portions and tasted good. One of the barracks was designed as a hospital, and skilled people like doctors and dentists worked with first-class equipment there. In the cafeteria, we could buy anything we wanted, even ice cream and sweets.

The camp was surrounded by a large and solid barbed-wire fence, and the camp's own police force kept a close eye so no one could come inside or leave the camp. If we were caught sneaking out, we had to pay ten, fifteen, or twenty dollars, all depending on how long our 'register of sins' were. We always thought twice before trying, because there was so much we could use our money on other than this. The north side of the camp bordered on the Maple Leaf Stadium, and this was a weak spot. It had a wooden fence which was very high and impossible to get over it, so no guards stayed much in the area. Some of the chaps had discovered this little fact, and one evening they went over there to saw a hole in the fence. They put a door in as well. For a long, long time they used this little door when they wanted to get in and out of the camp. The military police discovered the door in the end. One evening, when they knew their catch would be significantly high in number, they went in force and waited. When the boys showed up, one after another was caught and sent straight to a detention cell. Ironically, the camp police also had as much authority over their work outside the camp as inside. They went on the razz every week in Toronto, and drove to restaurants frequented by Norwegians. If they found anyone intoxicated or making trouble in the city (usually both), they were caught without further ado and brought back to the camp to sleep it off.

The Norwegians, at first, were very popular in Toronto. However, wherever Norwegians go, alcohol and trouble tend to follow. After a while, the Canadians grew more sceptical towards us. From what I know though, nothing ever got as far as newspaper headlines, Canadian girls being advised to stay away from dances we arranged, or banned from showing themselves Norwegians in uniform in public. Quite the contrary, we were more than welcome in Canadian homes, and spent many evenings with Canadian families. Naturally, it was the daughter of the household that was of most interest to us. Most Canadian girls were sweet and charming. They were nice to talk to and easy to get along with. When we started to speak of skiing or sailing they didn't quite follow us, though. It was not difficult to keep the conversation going, even when we occasionally used very long and clumsy sentences to make ourselves understood. They helped us find the right words, and I am sure that many of us have the Canadian girls to thank for improving our English.

The Norwegian Air Force was administered from 341 Churchstreet, about 15 minutes from Little Norway. Camp commander Lt-Col Ole Reistad had his offices here. This was the place where I would be meeting him upon arriving in Toronto. I showed up early in the morning and quickly discovered I was not the only morning bird. Five or six others had already taken their place outside the building, all of them of about the same, young age as me. It didn't take long until we were chatting away. We had all arrived in Toronto the day before. One of them had come by the same route as myself, from Montreal. Three others had worked in New York and arrived to volunteer. Another had travelled all the way around the world, and just arrived from San Francisco. Another had partly walked and driven from Portland, USA. He spoke a little sloppily, so I guessed he was a Norwegian-American. He told me he was born in Trondheim by Norwegian parents, but they had left for America when he was very young.

Our conversation was interrupted when the door opened and we were showed into Ole Reistad's office. He wanted to greet us, and wished us a warm welcome to Little Norway and Canada. He asked for our names, and showed keen interest in how we had managed to get ourselves to Toronto.

'We need all the people we can get,' he said, 'because these days a whole lot of men are needed to keep the Air Force in good shape. I'm sure you all want to be pilots, but remember that not all can be up there. Each of you has to do the best you can in a role which is right for you. Every man is equally important.'

We would hear these words more than once from Reistad, and my own hopes of becoming a pilot sank a little every time he spoke them. I already knew that each airplane needed about ten men on the ground. I had problems seeing why I might be chosen to fly these machines. However, I was firm in my decision to work hard towards the ultimate goal—learning to fly.

After this first interview with Reistad, things moved swiftly. First, we were enrolled in the military and each of us got his own military number. After

Little Norway, Toronto. You can see the Maple Leaf stadium in the background. (*Finn Eriksrud's collection*)

<u>Harold Odman</u>

As Eriksrud suspected, Odman was indeed a Norwegian-American. In the original book from 1945, Eriksrud calls him 'Harald', though his official records refer to him as 'Harold'—likely an Anglo-American twist to make it more palatable. Odman was born on 25 August 1919 in Trondheim, Norway. His parents were Sverre August Odman and Kirsti Odman. They moved to the United States when Harold was only three years old. They settled in Silverton, Oregon, on the west coast. He grew up in Silverton and went through the American school system. He finished high school and two years of study at Angel College in Oregon. He was educated as an accountant. In 1941, he got his civilian pilot's license and had about 50 hours in the air before he decided to sign up to the Norwegian forces. He was an eager boy scout throughout his childhood, and won several medals in rifle shooting competitions. He also enjoyed football (soccer), basketball, and swimming. Odman volunteered during the summer of 1941, and was accepted on 27 June 1941 in the same class as Finn Eriksrud. He followed Eriksrud to Emsdale in the summer, and then to Medicine Hat in Alberta from December 1941 to April 1942. Their entire spell at Little Norway lasted from August 1941 to April 1942. Odman might have been a little cocky due to his previous flying experience, as his instructor's assessment of his performance indicates:

> Average. Has achieved good results. Very over-confident in the air and very sure of himself. Very interested in flying.

After Medicine Hat, Odman returned to Toronto for an advanced flying course. In the late summer of 1942, he was sent to No. 31 General Reconnaissance School, where he flew Avro Ansons. Odman did not settle down: perhaps he was as impatient as Eriksrud lets on, for he was after some time sent back to Toronto to start fighter—instead of bomber—training. He became a sergeant in the Army Air Service. Odman left Toronto 4 January 1943. He joined 61 OTU at Rednal and Montford Bridge. In April 1943, he was finally ready to fly Spitfires with No. 332 Squadron at North Weald, Essex.

that first day, I became just another number, like everybody else. Then we were vaccinated. I am far from happy about having needles stuck in my arm, and I had already been vaccinated in Stockholm four months earlier, and brought evidence to prove it. I explained this to the doctor at Little Norway, and told him that I was more than fine where vaccinations were concerned. It was simply a waste of time for him to vaccinate me. In response, he assured me that he had plenty of time, and it didn't matter what I had done or had not done. So, the needle went in. I was comforted by the fact that I would most likely not get a fever or be bedridden, as had been the case in Stockholm the first time around. My arm was very sore and tender afterwards, and it didn't make all those drills with a weapon any more comfortable later on.

Next up was delivery of uniforms at the depot. We walked in our civilian clothes, and an hour later came back outside in full military dress. From war-paint to steel helmets and weapons—it was all there. I was finally in uniform. I was very proud walking out of the depot in my new battledress with a steel helmet on my head, a rifle on my arm, and a big blue backpack filled up to the brim. We were now going out to the training area at Centre Island to learn the basics of military behaviour and discipline. It turned out that my class had already been at it for a week already, so yours truly and Harold Odman, the Norwegian-American I had met at Reistad's, had a bit of catching up to do. That first evening, we found ourselves a spare room and available bunks. Harold took the lower bunk, I took the upper one.

The next morning we were awakened by someone's awful idea of music. It turned out to be the reveille. I do not like to get out of bed the minute I wake up, so I decided not do it this time either. I did find it a bit odd that everyone else jumped out of bed at once and stood by their bedsides. I on the other hand turned the other way, and tried to go back to sleep. I didn't get much more. A sergeant came roaring into the room, pulled the blanket off of me, and asked if I had ever been taught normal behaviour for a human being. I listened to him for a few minutes, and when his flood of words had finally died out, I tried to explain to him that this was my first day of basic training. I continued to tell him that from now I would be a good boy, and stand by my bedside when he showed up in the morning. We had one hour to wash up, eat breakfast, polish our shoes, do our beds, and mop the floor. For a while the hour was almost up by the time we got to breakfast, but once we into the habit, a good amount of time was left to eat.

At eight o' clock, it was time for the drill command. Harold and I were placed at the back. We were to join the others for military parade. We had trouble following the corporal in charge so he gave up on us for the meantime and promised to show us how it was done later that afternoon. We were seated on the lawn, looking at the others marching and turning. They did this until noon, after which there was an hour's rest. Then it was back to these drill commands, and again more parading. After that we were given lessons about weapons, and at the end of the day we had an hour of gymnastics. It felt extremely good to have a bath after such days, and we could have as many as we wanted, too. After all, it was only about 40 m down to the lake. During those first days, both Harold and I were feeling much too stiff in our bodies to even think of leaving camp. Once we had finished with the parades and training, we simply dove into our bunks. We didn't even have time to think about how wonderful the day had been before we fell asleep.

As the days came and went, I got used to life as a recruit. I vividly remember all those inspections, where some sergeant walked around and looked into the barrel of our rifles. If he found just the slightest bit of dust, another hour of cleaning was ordered. There were about a hundred men at the school while I was there, and practically all of them had sent in an application to join the Air Force. Everyone with the right qualifications, which meant being qualified for university or college education, was closely examined by a doctor before being accepted for combat. Many of us were very nervous about this medical 'test'. We had heard rumours it was important not to have high blood pressure, so everyone ate a copious amount of oranges for weeks before the test took place. Whether this helped or not, I have no idea, but I guess the important thing was that we thought it did. The test was not as hard as it was rumoured to be, not for a person with normal functionality. Our lungs were tested by blowing up a column of mercury, and keeping the mercury up for 60 seconds or so. Our eyesight was tested to see if we were colour-blind, and if it was sharp enough. After that was over, we were put up against a wall and X-rayed. We were thoroughly checked out by every possible means.

There was also an intelligence test involved. We had to answer a lot of basic questions in very little time. I was really nervous about this test after I had

Shooting practise in Canada, Little Norway. Finn Eriksrud stands closest to the photographer. (*Finn Eriksrud's collection*)

A Curtiss Hawk and a Northrop A-17 at Little Norway in foggy conditions. (*Finn Eriksrud's collection*)

taken it. My impression was that I did not perform very well. I got even more nervous when I was called back in to do the test again. I sat down at the table once more, and started to answer the same questions. This time I did much better. It was very nice of the Air Force to give me a second chance, even if I didn't really understand the point of serving someone the same intelligence test twice. I enquired further on the subject, telling them I had taken the test twice, and asking whether I had been completely hopeless the first time around. However, after further investigation it turned out that the entire affair was a misunderstanding, and that I had not done so poorly on my first test.

This first introduction to army life concluded with a gathering at which Ole Reistad was present. We were all anxious about this too. Reistad, though, seemed to be pleased with our results, and gave a little speech in our honour. Once again, he touched upon the reality that not all of us could become pilots, and the extent to which this position was sought after. It was the pilot that brought results to the table and got the credit, but we had to remember, he told us, that each man had to do his duty, wherever that may be. Not one of us could be spared, and the Air Force needed every one of us to run smoothly.

After this meeting, we would be told which one of us had been accepted into flying school. Only forty of us were going to be let in, so tensions were running high. We tried to calculate which of us would be accepted. Discussions ran wild, and it was curious that we tried to comfort and support each other. Finally, the list was published, and both Harold and I were among the lucky few. We had reached one of our major goals.

We then moved to the heart of Little Norway. A busy time was ahead of us, we realised this at once. We had a tonne of books to read: navigation, radio, meteorology, engines, weapons, and geography. At the same time, our schedule began at eight in the morning and finished at four in the afternoon, with an hour rest in the middle of the day.

We spent most of the coming five months studying, but we still had drill commands and gymnastics. This was in the middle of August, so the weather was nice and warm. It was therefore hard to study in the afternoon, obviously. Another rumour told us that the five lowest graduates would be dropped from the programme, so that kept us on our toes.

It was at this time that I bought a car. When I arrived in Canada, I had applied to be compensated for my travel expenses all the way to Toronto. This application was accepted. I put all the money in the bank, and originally decided to leave it there until the end of the war. However, one afternoon I was in the city with a friend, and he was looking to buy a car. We tried one car after another, and after a while I ended up buying one myself. When I got back to camp that afternoon, the bank account was empty, but the car was mine. I got much pleasure from this car for as long as it lasted. I had been driving it around for about six months when I ran into a big lorry, and that was the end of that.

A foggy day in Toronto's Island Airport, the training ground for the Norwegians of Little Norway. (*Finn Eriksrud's collection*)

Finn Eriksrud in front of a Northrop A-17. (*Finn Eriksrud's collection*)

Harold and I drove all around Ontario on our time off. One weekend we went down to the Niagara Falls to look at this wonder that we had heard so much about. It was indeed an impressive sight, and it was an incredible amount of water falling off that gigantic cliff. But for some reason I was a bit disappointed. I don't know why, but I guess my expectations were too high. Other weekends we visited villages close by. There was nothing to do in Toronto on Sundays or holidays. Theatres and cinemas were all closed. No places to go.

Exams were closing in on me, and things sped up fast. There was less and less time for anything other than studying. I stayed up, studying long into the evenings. I specifically had trouble with my weapons' studies, since we had to learn all names of all the parts in English. With only two days to go until the exam, I felt I knew as little about weapons as when I had first started. I had no choice but to get hold of the different parts and weapons and lock myself into a classroom. I stayed there for 24 hours straight, learning the names of every part and mechanism.

Some pupils started to doubt their own abilities to become pilots, and thought they wouldn't make it. They were comforted by the teachers, who told them there was nothing magical about the heavens above. The air was just like water, they told them. It also acted like water. They were sure that this was something most of us could relate to. Harold was among those who walked around camp doubting his own abilities. It was later proven that he was a very skilful pilot. Harold's Norwegian was not yet up to par, and he had problems understanding how to address different people in the proper way. Every time he made a mistake, laughter broke out. He approached the teachers the wrong way, and had other issues with speaking in general. When later on we were sent to an English school, it was his turn to laugh as we tried to explain matters in his language.

All of us passed the exam, and we would now start flying in earnest. The very next day, each of us got a parachute, packed our bags, and left for Emsdale.

7

First Solo Flight

Emsdale is a small village located about 300 km north of Toronto. The airfield itself is situated about 20 km from Emsdale, and is completely surrounded by thick forest. We arrived there in the afternoon. Both ground crew and pupils had to sleep in tents, as there were only two buildings erected on site—a hangar and a house used for the officers' mess. The aircraft, Fairchild Cornells, had already been flown up from Toronto, and were neatly parked on the apron. They were low-wing monoplanes with an engine of 180 horse power. They had two cockpits, one in front of the other. In the front was seated the pupil with his stick and instruments, and behind him the instructor with the same equipment. The aircraft could be flown just as well from either position. Each instructor got two pupils to teach. We started to fly the day after our arrival.

The instructors had a thankless and tough task. For hours on end, they showed us how to land the Cornell. It looked easy when they did it, but when we tried the plane just came down in every way possible but for the right one.

The instructor sat behind me, wondering what would happen next time I tried to land. They would more that often let us do the landing ourselves, but sometimes, when they saw things were going horribly wrong, they had to take over. I would hear a simple 'I have control' over the radio, upon which a sigh of relief would invariably follow, for I usually saw for myself that I was coming in all wrong. However, do not think that the instructor was a nice, patient, sweet man who easily put up with his pupil's gambling with both of their lives. When the aircraft had finally landed after a bad landing, we knew what was coming. We were given a detailed lesson of the instructor's impressive vocabulary. 'Did you really think you could learn to fly? You don't even have the skill to keep the proper speed!' The instructor had seen hopeless flying in the past, but what we were doing took the bloody cake. He had done everything in his power to teach us to fly, but we did not even have the reactions of normal human beings. If he hadn't been there with us, we would

Temporary housing at Emsdale—basically, tents! (*Finn Eriksrud's collection*)

One of the few real houses at Emsdale. (*Finn Eriksrud's collection*)

all have flown into the trees with our eyes open. 'I give up on all of you,' he said. Most of us lost whatever confidence we had left.

I thought much about what the instructor had told us, and genuinely felt we all of us were unfairly treated. We couldn't really be that hopeless, could we? It was then that we got mad. We would show these instructors what we were really made of. The result was that we got a grip on our flying, and performed much better. This happened often. We had periods where nothing worked out, and everything looked bleak, then suddenly the next day, we were doing the opposite and performing well once more.

The instructors would give us praise, if you could call it that. Not all instructors managed to hold back until they were back on terra firma. Some of them got so angry that they walked out on the wing and gave us a knock on the head! It's clear to me that this method had an adverse effect. The pupil just got even more nervous than before, and couldn't perform well at all. Sometimes, the pupil pulled the short straw. This happened when Harold and Blommen were up in the air doing aerobatics. Blommen was one of the instructors, and this was the nickname we gave him. So, Harold was told to do a roll. He turned the aircraft on its back, and while he was upside down he felt his stick freezing up on him. At the same time, he heard some commotion from the back seat. He turned around and found Blommen lying in the top of the cockpit looking rather helpless. Harold eventually managed to free the stick, and turned the aircraft the right way up again. When he asked whether he should do any more aerobatics, he was told to land at once. When Blommen finally got down again, he was bleeding badly and felt very poorly. We didn't dare suggest that he had, in fact, forgotten to strap himself in before the flight.

I was making slow progress. My landings were no longer fatally dangerous, and the instructor had less and less to complain about. I now managed to land the aircraft on my own, but it was still good to know that if I got it wrong, someone was there to take over. I had just done my third landing one day and was taxiing back to holding point when the instructor came on the radio and told me to do the next one alone.

At first I was a little shocked. Sooner or later I had to fly alone, that was for certain, but I had not prepared myself for this being so soon. I didn't feel remotely confident that I could pull it off on my own, but if the instructor thought I could do it, well, I couldn't really say no. I had to give it my best shot.

I told my instructor I would manage the solo flight, though my trembling voice gave me away. The instructor jumped off the wing, and there I was—all alone with 180 horse power. I got that strange sensation in my stomach, as I did each time I went ski jumping back home, progressing onto bigger and bigger hills. I broke out in a sweat and my hands were shaking, but it was too late to turn back now. Many of the other pupils had already done their

Finn Eriksrud in front of an Avro Anson. The photo might have been taken at Emsdale. (*Finn Eriksrud's collection*)

solos, and everyone had come out in one piece. I had also done my previous three landings with no major issues. There was no more time to think of these matters, as I was waved up to the runway. Then the signal came; all clear for take-off.

Alright, it was now or never. I put all my worries to one side as I tried to keep the aircraft on the centre line. The speed increased, and soon the wheels left the runway. It felt very strange being up in the air alone, especially given how far from sure I was about my abilities. But everything seemed to be going well, I did what I had been told, and slowly my confidence started to come back to me. Such an odd sensation, flying around in the skies alone! I felt so happy and light-hearted. I flew around for a good while and felt as free as a bird. I had to come down again some time, though, and that was when the old nerves returned to my stomach. When it came down to it, it was much easier to take off and fly around than it was to land. I had to trust myself this time around. I circled the airfield a couple of times, and saw my instructor observing me from the ground. He must have wondered how I would do as well. I flew some more circles, just to gather my courage. I repeated the procedures in my own head one last time, and then prepared for landing. My approach was quite good. My speed was decent and I thought I was safe. However, my height was wrong. I was too high. I simply fell from the sky those last metres down the ground. The undercarriage made it through, though, as the aircraft jumped up and down going down the runway. It stopped in good time before the end of the strip, and I sighed with relief. It wasn't really that hard to land the aircraft. The instructor came towards me, and congratulated me. He told me that my solo flight would be the last thing I did that day as he didn't want me to become too cocky.

The next day, I was back to doing circuits with my instructor again. My hours in the air kept increasing. I had now got as far as aerobatics. First up was spinning. The instructor took the aircraft up to 6,000 feet and pulled the throttle off while keeping the nose high. Then he pulled the stick harder towards him, and gave right rudder. The aircraft got thrown over on its back and started to spin around and around, with what felt to me as ever increasing speed. At the start I had no idea what was going on, and didn't know what was up or down. It felt as though it was the Earth that was spinning. I also started to feel slightly worried as we approached the ground very quickly and still spinning. The instructor's voice calmed me down though. He simply told me that we'd done a few spins now, and that the spinning would stop. Quite right. We made half a turn and the aircraft came out of the spin and into a dive. A little pull on the stick and we were back on course. Then it was my turn. We climbed up to 6,000 feet again, and I did what I had been told. I was more than a little on edge, so didn't really get the hang of it. I had to go for another try, and this time was successful. I also understood more of what was going on. I even managed to count the rounds we did, going down. After three of them I was told to exit the spin the same way the instructor had done before me. It all went well.

In the coming weeks, I did a lot of this type of flying. I started to feel more and more at home in the air.

We also had to learn to navigate. We had already been taught the theory behind it, and now it was time to try it out in real life. At first, we flew short trips with the instructor so as not to start by getting lost. We were often told that if we did not know where we were, we could not get nervous and start to fly around in circles. We just had to stay calm and carry on. If we kept a steady course we would eventually reach something of recognition. A mountain, a lake, a railway line, or something that we could find on the map. If we did not deviate from our course and kept an eye on our speed, we should theoretically know where to look on a map for an idea of where we were flying.

This sounded like a cinch, but the following day it was my turn to realize that this was easier said than done. Some of the pupils had already flown their first navigation exercises when I was first up. The sun was shining in a clear, blue sky. I found my heading on the map, and calculated the time I would be using. The whole trip would take me two hours and 15 minutes. I started around two in the afternoon, circled up to the correct altitude over the airfield and headed out. These parts of Canada were sparsely populated. All I could see were small lakes and large forests. A long way ahead I spotted smoke moving on the ground. It had to be a train, and this was confirmed when I crossed over it later on. I next flew over a few farms and small roads. I could see how the people stopped doing their work when I flew over. I don't think they often saw aircraft flying over them. So, it was without problem that I reached the first goal of the exercise. Right then, navigation was nothing to write home about, very easy stuff. I also found my next goal easily, and then it was time to head back. Everything had been running so smoothly that I relaxed my navigational focus. I was thrilled to the core with myself and my flying prowess, and even began to think it boring to just fly in a straight line all the time. Why not do a few loops instead? Obviously, this was against orders. I was sent up to do navigation, not aerobatics. But, I was the only flying object for miles and miles around, so who would know? I climbed to 2,000 feet, and started to fool around. This was so much better than flying straight and level for hours. Just when I was doing my second loop, the engine started coughing. I instantly got flustered, as this was no place to make an emergency landing. Just trees, trees, and more trees. The engine ran rougher by the minute, and I had to lose altitude to keep it from stopping. I got scared, and sweat was running down my back. I checked the instruments again and again, but I couldn't remember if they were right or wrong. Then the engine stopped. The propeller was just wind-milling crisp Canadian air. The trees crept up on me. Should I jump out or actually try for a landing? My whole body was shaking with fear, and sweat was dripping from my face, not just my back. Just a few moments ago, I had been so full of myself, without a care in the world. Now it looked as though the fun would be over. I would never have a single worry again, because I would be a goner within minutes. I pulled myself together, and tried to remember what to do if the engine stopped. Why would it have stopped? Then it struck me—I couldn't expect the engine to run if it didn't have any fuel to run on. I flicked a switch, and the engine burst into life again. It couldn't have come soon enough. The altitude was 650 feet.

Owing to this distraction, I had completely forgotten what heading I had been flying in for the last few minutes. I could not be far off course, though. I climbed up to 6,500 feet to get a better view of my surroundings. It didn't last long before I saw a large lake which fitted nicely in with what I was looking at on my map. I calculated my course to the airfield on this map based on this lake. However, the more I flew the more concerned I became. Somehow, I knew that I was flying the wrong way. I simply could not match anything I saw with the map I had at my disposal. I started to sweat again, as the clock quickly ticked towards four in the afternoon. It started to get dark. As far as I could see, there were only forests and small lakes. There was no sign of life anywhere. I spotted another lake to starboard, and again checked my map. It looked like the same lake. I flew over it, then started to circle to make sure I had found the right one. To my disbelief, it dawned on me after a few circuits that this lake did not in fact match anything on my map. I had to admit that I was completely lost. Oh boy, was I in trouble now. I broke out in a cold sweat, and my stomach span like a carousel. Without any kind of plan I flew to one lake after the next and checked with my map. I could no longer make even an educated guess as to my position.

The situation was becoming increasingly critical. It was getting gradually darker, and I started to contemplate landing before all went pitch black on me. The fuel needle was sinking lower by the minute. I could still keep flying for another 40 minutes, but that would be it. What would happen if I tried an emergency landing? I had no food with me either. Even if I got down in one piece, how long would it take for anyone to locate me? How long would I have to walk to find people? What chance would I have if I broke my leg or injured myself during the landing? Maybe I had better chances of survival if I jumped out, using my parachute? I didn't really want to abandon my aircraft either. There was a first aid kit at the back, close to the tail section. No, I decided to stick with the aircraft. I kept thinking about my options as I aimlessly flew around.

Then I spotted a light moving on my port side. Perhaps a car? I flew towards what I had observed. It disappeared for a moment, but popped right back up again. Quite right, it was moving. It was surely a car. A couple of minutes later I flew right over it. My confidence gradually came back to me, and I felt a sigh

Emsdale. (*Finn Eriksrud's collection*)

of sweet relief. All I had to do was to follow the road, and that wasn't very hard as the white line separating the two driving directions was easy to spot. Sooner or later, I simply had to reach some kind of town that was marked on my map. If I didn't reach an airfield in time, I could at least jump out, aiming to land on the road or in a field. My eyes shifted between the road and the fuel gauge. I wondered if it was 100-per-cent accurate. If it was correct, I could fly on for another 15 minutes.

I saw several cars driving down there, and couldn't help but think how lucky they all were, these people driving. They all knew where they were heading, and if they didn't, all they had to do was ask someone. It was a bit more complicated to do so up in an aircraft. There I was, in this machine above their heads; how very controlled and easy it must have seemed to them. If only they knew how helpless and scared I was.

I was quietly speculating to myself about how this all would end when I suddenly saw several lights ahead. Little by little, more of them cropped up. It just had to be a town. Finding out which town was of the essence. This was far from easy. I circled over it looking for things I could recognise. If it had been broad daylight outside, it would have been so much easier, and I could have aimed for the train station and its signals. I did have a slight suspicion I had seen the church before. Could this be Huntsville? If this truly was Huntsville, I was only 15 minutes away from the airfield. When I spotted lights from a cinema, I flew over to get a better look. The board read, *Fantasia, Walt Disney*. I was no longer in doubt: the cinema's name was Rex. I knew this, too. I had actually been there two days ago. Even if it was dark outside, it was easy to find the airfield from here. Minutes later, I spotted the landing lights. I looked at the fuel gauge again—10 litres left. This would do.

I had never done a night landing before, so I was very tense about it. I was also very glad it was dark enough for no one to really witness my landing. The undercarriage didn't crack this time either, so no one had to know anything. Except for me. I was so happy to be back that I wasn't annoyed at my mistakes, either. I can safely say that that landing was the worst I had ever done, or would ever do. Enough said.

I got out of the aircraft and reported to the office, where the head of the instructors was waiting for me. He was not in the best of moods, that was easy to see. He kept thumping his fingers on the wooden desk. I realised that there was no use in trying to cook up some bogus story like I had originally planned. I came clean. I told him about my aerobatics, and how I had been flying around with no plan, not keeping the aircraft straight and level. The next day, the mechanic reported back that there were only six litres of fuel left in the tanks—enough for five minutes of flying. It did not improve my position one bit, and I was confined to camp for five weeks. I didn't really need more punishment, in any case, for I had learned a lot.

An Avro Anson photographed by Fridtjof Giørtz. (*Fridtjof Giørtz's collection*)

The weather worsened as we approached autumn. It got really unstable. We had many days of rain, so much flying was cancelled. We put the time to good use, anyway. We were taught theory such as Morse code and other signalling methods. We also spent a good deal of time on aircraft recognition. The ability to distinguish our own from enemy aircraft was vital. We were still newbies, and not very good at it. When we later arrived in England, and were warned about pilots shooting down their own mates because they couldn't see the difference, we understood the seriousness of this lesson. We got up to scratch at the speed of lightning.

We also spent many hours in the Link Trainer. It reacted just like an aircraft when we moved the controls. It even went into a spin if the speed dropped too low. It was generally used to teach the pupils blind flying—flying on instruments. When you're dropping into clouds during the night, obviously there is no external help available. If we didn't have these instruments, it would be impossible to know which way the aircraft was going in comparison to earth. In the Link Trainer, when you are strapped in with a cap draped over your head, the instruments are the only thing you see. The pupil gets his orders from the instructor, seated at a table close by and following the Link Trainer's movements, which he reads on a piece of paper before him. When the training is over, the pupil walks over to the instructor, who then points out what mistakes the pupil made and so on.

The Link Trainer saved us a lot of time and money. Without this equipment,

Finn Eriksrud wrote the following on the back: 'From the training camp at Muskoka, Canada 1941.' From the left: Reidar Døvle Moe, pilot of No. 333 Squadron, A-Flight, Catalina; Leif Erik Hulthun, pilot of the English No. 76 Squadron, Halifax bomber, shot down during a mission to Kassel on the night of 22/23 October 1943, his nineteenth sortie; Rolf Leithe, pilot of No. 333 Squadron, B-Flight, Mosquito, killed while test flying on 22 March 1945; Fridtjof Giørtz, pilot of Bomber Command and the Stockholm route; Kjell Tvedt, pilot, Spitfire; Finn Eriksrud, pilot of No. 333 Squadron, B-Flight, Mosquito, shot down in combat with German aircraft outside Bomlø on 18 December 1943, POW in Germany together with navigator Erling Victor Johanssen; Axel Reidar Eikemo, pilot of No. 333 Squadron, B-Flight, killed in action on 1 August 1944 during an attack on a submarine; Carl Thorleif Johnsen, pilot of No. 330 Squadron, Sunderland; Niels Eckhoff, pilot of the English No. 76 Squadron, Halifax bomber, killed on the night of 3/4 October 1943 over the Ruhr. (*Finn Eriksrud's collection*)

instruction for blind flying had to be taken in the air. If you have done a course on the Link Trainer, you could strap yourself into a real flying machine and fly on nothing but your instruments through the thickest of clouds without trouble. We spent hours and hours in the Link Trainer before being put into active service. I think we had up to 50 or 60 hours in it.

The Link Trainer is very realistic, and gives you the sensation of sitting in a real aircraft. The following story tells you this much.

A Canadian was using the Link Trainer to practise his flying, when he suddenly lost control and the Link Trainer started to spin. The Canadian did everything he could to get it out of the spin, but did not succeed. When he took a quick glance at his altimeter, he saw that he was only a few hundred feet above ground level. He quickly opened the door and threw himself out and onto the floor, subsequently breaking his leg in the fall.

After a rainy autumn, December was approaching, and it started to get quite cold living in a tent. All our aircraft were covered in thick layers of ice and frost on the wings in the mornings. The days got shorter as well. I had about 100 hours of flying time on the Cornell by this stage. On the same day as the attack on Pearl Harbour, we packed up our gear and left Emsdale.

A Temporary Fear of Flying

The journey to Medicine Hat never seemed to end. We had seats in these nice Pulman carriages. Each night, a muscular African-American stepped inside and turned our carriage into a sleeping carriage. The journey took about three days. I never knew the Canadian prairie was so enormous. We did anything to make time pass. Playing cards or reading books. When we looked outside, it was the same old scenery. Wavy prairie grounds as far as the eye could see.

Each time the train stopped, we rushed out to get more books or sweets. Time and time again we told each other that it felt as though we had just visited this station. They were that similiar.[1]

Our training had until now been under Norwegian instructors and control. Now, our group of pilots-to-be was separated into two distinct groups. One group would become bombers, the other fighters. Both of these courses would now take place under British command, using the English language.

Medicine Hat

Medicine Hat was and still is an active airfield, located two nautical miles south-west of the town of Medicine Hat in Alberta, Canada. When Finn Eriksrud arrived, it was part of the British Commonwealth Air Training Plan for the No. 34 Service Flying Training School. The SFTFS was open from 8 April 1941 to 17 November 1944.

One of Eriksrud's best friends after the Second World War was Harald Hartmann, a Catalina pilot with No. 333 Squadron's A-Flight at Woodhaven. He also travelled to Medicine Hat for his training and arrived there on 2 August of 1942, four months before Eriksrud arrived.

The base was under the command of Wg Cdr Colin Scragg, an Englishman and strict disciplinarian, according to Hartmann. The latter felt some of Scragg's ideas were old-fashioned and too 'by the book', but the Norwegian had to admit, Scragg gave him a first-class education. The Norwegians were treated equally to British pupils, and they were expected to look smart and be on their toes.

When Hartman first came to Medicine Hat, the entire class stood to attention while Scragg inspected them. By the looks of it, Scragg had memorised the names, service numbers, and photographs of all of his pupils before they even had set foot on camp. Hartmann further recounts,

> Scrabb stopped by one of the young pupils and asked:
> 'Private Jameson, do you have any questions?'
> The boy had no questions, but he most likely got the feeling he should have had a question ready. Scragg was far from done with him.
> 'What is the time, Pte Jameson?'
> Pte Jameson thought it was an easy question to answer. He looked at his watch.
> '10.28, sir.'
> Scragg had already looked at his watch, and replied quickly:
> 'Wrong, it's not. It's 10.29. Get your watch synchronized.'[2]

Norwegians, Air Force Training Camp (FTL, Flyvåpnenes Treningsleir), Class No. 2/twin-engine aircraft, Medicine Hat. December 1941 – April 1942: Niels Stockfleth D. Eckhoff; Reidar Askel Eikemo; Finn Eriksrud; Fredtjov Sæverud Giørtz; Leif Eric Woodrow Hulthin; Harald Jensen; Carl Thorleif Johnsen; Rolf Leithe; Ole Tobias Mehn-Andersen; Reidar Døvle Moe; Harold Odman; Tore Stensrud; Kjell Wilhelm Tvedt; Andreas Hofgaard Wyller; Bror Lars Burman Aarflot.

Both Harold and I were sent to become bombers, learning to fly twin-engine aircraft. The training base we were going to was located far out in West Canada, as far as the Rocky Mountains. The closest town was called Medicine Hat. The British had earlier on in the war moved most of their training bases to Canada and South Africa to avoid any trouble from the Luftwaffe. The result was that English bases were scattered all over. Our training camp had Canadian guards. From time to time, there was some friction between them and British pilots. In my opinion, this stemmed from the fact that the latter were popular with the girls in town, having arrived from exotic Britain. One evening, a fight broke out in Medicine Hat between the Canadians and the British. There were a few Norwegians around as well, and they couldn't let such an opportunity pass them by. The Norwegians were initially unsure as to who to side with in the fight. In the end, they decided to help the Canadians. As thanks, we could from then on walk in and out of camp as we pleased, while the guards kept a strict eye on the British, reporting them for the slightest of

Chilly weather at Medicine Hat, Canada. (*Finn Eriksrud's collection*)

Wg Cdr Colin Scragg speaks at a gathering at Medicine Hat. (*Fridtjof Giørtz's collection*)

late-comings. As Norwegians, we also had other privileges at this base. Every Saturday there was an inspection. All buttons, shoes, and clothes had to be perfectly clean, and the bed had to be in a certain order. We didn't have the same equipment as the British, and the sergeant who made the inspection had no knowledge of what the Norwegian rules required of us to do, while we ourselves had absolutely no clue what the British rules were. This all ended up with us leading an easy life at camp, while the British pupils had to sit and polish those buttons like never before.

We arrived in Medicine Hat on 23 December 1942. We celebrated Christmas the Norwegian way, or tried to at least. We got ourselves a Christmas tree, and brought gifts with us from Little Norway. There were plenty of presents from Norwegian-Americans living in the States as well. No one wanted to sing any carols though. Most of us stayed in bed thinking about what we had accomplished in the past year, and what we had done the previous Christmas when were all back home. Where would the next Christmas be? So there wasn't much Christmas spirit going around. There was no snow outside, either.

It was during those special holidays that homesickness quickly engulfed me. Christmas, Easter, 17th of May, or mid-summer. Apart from on these dates, there were so many things going on that thoughts of family and Norway just stayed in the back of my head.

The British didn't celebrate Christmas like we did. Their big day is the first day of Christmas. A massive dinner was served at the base. We ate two large meals that day, one in the early afternoon in the mess and another one in the evening when all of us had been invited to family homes in Medicine Hat. The dinner in the mess was very funny. The British have a custom of trading places in the course of the day, the officers serving the lower ranks and so on. So there we were, enjoying things while the officers ran around and served us everything we asked for. In the evening, Harold and I had dinner with a female teacher in the town.

On the second day of Christmas, we were back to our daily routines. First up was a month long theory course. It was basically the same as what we had been through before, only this time they went deeper into the material, and the lectures were in English. None of us were very good at English yet, so we all wondered how we would manage the written exam. Our instructors were well aware of the problem though, and made sure we knew that if there were issues with the language or things we could not find the words to explain, Norwegian would have to do. One of us had particular difficulty in the exam, but he did his absolute best and wrote in English anyway. The next day, one of the teachers showed up and asked what language he had written his paper in. He could, as an English native, confirm that what the Norwegian had written was not English. Just to be sure, he had checked if it might perhaps have been some Norwegian dialect, but it wasn't that either. So what was it? But after a few hard knocks with the language, he too passed his exam.

I was now flying Airspeed Oxfords. This was a low-winged monoplane, with two engines and several instruments I had never seen before in my life. A handle I could not account for had also popped up in the cockpit. I used to stroll down to the hangar in the evenings to familiarise myself with the cockpit, even though we had been warned about touching anything. I remember one English pupil who couldn't control himself and wanted to touch everything. One evening, I was walking past the hangar with Harold when we saw one of the Oxfords slowly sinking towards the ground. Shortly afterwards, the terrified Englishman emerged from the aircraft. He had obviously tried one of those new handles and pulled the undercarriage up. He wasn't very popular with the chief instructor thereafter.

There was one, especially unforgivable sin: landing without wheels. It should, in theory, have been difficult to commit such an error, since two red lights shone brightly in the cockpit for as long as the wheels were retracted—these didn't change to green until the wheels were out and locked in their position. On top of these lights, a horn would blast away if we reduced the throttle when we came in to land, at which point most of us would realise that something was wrong and went for another go-around. In spite of all these warnings, it was not unknown for aircraft to come in and land nicely on their bellies.

Incidents at Medicine Hat

Another incident at Medicine Hat is vividly remembered by Fridtjof Giørtz after the war. One pupil let an Oxford's engines run after landing—a normal procedure, in case someone else was going up immediately afterwards. But he also forgot to put on the parking brake on: suddenly, the aircraft started to move on its own towards down the runway. One mechanic noticed the fugitive Oxford, and got four others to help him chase down the pilotless aircraft. Just moments before it was going to crash into the barracks, it made a 180-degree turn of its own accord, and came straight towards the four chaps on its tail. It then made another 180-degree turn and headed out towards the runway again. The Oxford kept going for some time before Andreas Wyller finally managed to get on board and shut it down. Onlookers had a hard time holding in their laughter.

Out here on the prairie I also began night flying. In the beginning, I didn't enjoy it very much, as it was very tricky to land in the dark. I could never get the hang of knowing my altitude, which resulted in many heavy landings. I eventually became more experienced and actually started to enjoy it. If the sky was clear and enough stars shone, I rarely felt better than when I was out flying around on my own.

Hartman mentions a specific, sports-related incident during his time at Medicine Hat. Everyone was expected to take part in the sports' events organised, and indeed most did. The Norwegians took part in every game arranged, and as hard as it was for Hartman to predict, they swept the table clear when it was time for the awards to be handed out: over and over again, a Norwegian was called up to claim his prize. The Brits took it well enough, but when a swimming competition was later held, it was strictly for the British. Hartman was of the opinion that the Norwegian boys were in better shape, and that this wasn't very fair on their Commonwealth friends. According to him, the Norwegians' superior skills at Medicine Hat had to do with Britain's poverty during the 1930s. This period's recession had hit Britain much harder than it did Norway, not forgetting that, up until the Americans and Russians joined in, the English had been fighting a war against Germany all on their own. They had been alone on the continent, in Africa, the Mediterranean, and even China, and had been pushed back on nearly all fronts—at Dunkirk, practically a whole army had vanished. Hartmann recounts that they were tough and held on, but that their physical resources had already been either put to the test or spent. Further still, the recruitment process in 1942 was, in all likelihood, less selective than before; the RAF was shorter of pilots than it was of aircraft. By the time Norway's youth was excelling both at sports and in the air at camps like Medicine Hat, Britain had, perhaps, already lost the majority of its most skilled pilots.

It was at Medicine Hat that I went through a period of being simply terrified of flying. When I was told to go up and do a few circuits, I tried to do as I was told, but the will was never there. I quickly gave up the tasks that were laid out before me. It was as though the aircraft and I no longer saw eye to eye. The aircraft was flying me, not the reverse. For example, if I was told to go up and do some sharp turns or use only one engine, I went up and just aimlessly flew around. I just couldn't get a grip and do what I was told. I don't really know what it was that I was so afraid of either. I never had this sense of fear and nervousness before. I didn't want to tell any of my friends about it, not even Harold, in whom I usually confided everything.

This dragged on for about a week until I went flying with my instructor one day. He quickly discovered that I did what he told me to do, but only barely, and without resolve. I also think I behaved very nervously, and he figured out that something was up. Luckily, he wasn't upset or annoyed with me. He simply showed me the ropes and told me to do them accordingly until he was satisfied. This lasted for over two hours. When it was all over, my fear of flying had disappeared, and I believed in myself once more.

I was once again eager to fly and enjoyed my time in the air for the rest of the course, which lasted well into April 1942. As it came to an end we were paraded around and given our wings, as testament that we truly were pilots. Of those of us who had entered the course, about 10 per cent had gone for various reasons. For a whole hour we stood there, swaying oh so gently in the wind. I have to confess, most of us had been out celebrating our wings a bit before the official ceremony. The English commander called us forward, and placed the wing badge on our chest.

Graduation

The 10th of April 1942 was a pivotal moment for our class. We were given our shiny wings. We had all the rights in the world to carry them on our uniforms from now on. We could finally call ourselves pilots.[3]

We were finally real pilots, with the rank of sergeant. I had reached my goal. I wasn't all done with training, though, as I had yet more learning to do before I could be sent to a squadron.

Gunnar Høverstad, Gunnar Randers, and Finn Eriksrud. Notice how Høverstad and Eriksrud's uniforms differ due to the distinction of Norway's Army Air Force from its Navy Air Force. *(Finn Eriksrud's collection)*

9

Final Steps at Prince Edward Island

The following and final course we had to go through was a general navigation school out on Prince Edward Island, located in St. Lawrence bay on the Canadian east coast. Here we would learn how to navigate, in theory and in practise. We were already pilots for all intents and purposes, but we also had to acquire navigational skills. For nine weeks—a time I look back on as one of the most intense yet most informative periods of my life—I learned all about a navigator's work and duties.

It is of great importance that pilots should learn plenty of navigation. If something were to happen to the navigator on board, it's imperative that the pilot can take over his duties and bring the aircraft back home. The pilot also has his own way of blaming everything on the poor navigator if the aircraft arrives at the wrong place, is late, or even is early. It doesn't matter how good the navigator is, though, if the pilot in charge does not keep a straight course, or for example forgets to maintain proper speed. We gained this experience on the course as navigators ourselves. If we had a pilot flying his given course to the exact detail, everything went well. If we didn't end up where we were supposed to end up, it was often the pilot's fault. However, we made mistakes too (as navigators) and blamed the pilot for things he hadn't done.

All of the flying on this course was done over the ocean. We flew for hours on end without seeing any land at all. Out there in the Atlantic, there are no landmarks to help us out. The most important information for finding out our exact location was the amount of time we had flown, the average speed of the aircraft, and the compass's orientation. There was one other factor involved, too—the aircraft's drift.

Even if the nose of the aircraft points in one direction, it is rare that the aircraft actually flies on this course. It only does so when the wind is coming from directly behind it or head on. If the wind comes in from either side of the aircraft, it will drift off course. There are therefore two movements: forwards, the direction in which the pilot is flying, and the direction in which the aircraft *actually* moves over the ocean. It's the navigator's responsibility to find this drift or angle between the course of the aircraft and the direction of the wind.

You find it with special equipment on board, usually placed at the nose of the aircraft over a window so the navigator can see the ocean.

At the end of the course we were introduced to photography and the use of the camera on board. We would use a large, heavy apparatus weighing at least 10 kg. The only way to get photographs was to hold the camera out of the window. The first time I took photo reconnaissance of a town, I flew with a pilot who seemed to want to make the trip as down to earth as possible. I did not find this out until afterwards, though, when we approached the town. I opened the windows and got the camera out into the strong wind, ready to photograph. Suddenly, the aircraft dropped its wing. If it wasn't for the fact that I had signed for the camera and would have to pay for it if something happened to it, I probably would have dropped it. As it was, I clung to it with my life.

The pilot kept dangerously throwing the aircraft this way and that in the sky. I could barely hang on, let alone take photographs. I managed to take a few photographs after much strain and effort, and decided to call it a day pretty quickly. When I got back with nothing but photographs of the wings and the heavens above to show my teachers, my grade suffered heavily. The pilot, on the other hand, thought everything was as it should be. He told me it was like this on real sorties.

There were enemy submarines in the St. Lawrence River in those days. We never had any explosives with us when were out flying, though. Those aircraft were so full of people that we couldn't take any bombs with us. However, we were told that if we saw any submarines, we were to act exactly as though we had them on board. The submarine crews would think we were attacking them as usual. This happened a few times, and the Germans dove away quickly. After a while it seemed the Germans caught on to what we were up to. One day, one of our aircraft dived down to attack, and all the Germans did was stand on the deck and wave as they roared past. This left a bitter taste in everyone's mouth.

Spare time at Prince Edward Island as recorded by Harald Hartmann

During our time off, we left the base for the capital of St. Lawrence Island, Charlottetown, to check out 'the local surroundings'. Like everywhere else, it was full of young girls who thought all these pilots were very exciting, especially those as strange to them as the Norwegians. Many friendly Canadians opened their homes to us. Some of them preferred their daughters to frequent strangers in the comfort of their parents' home, rather than by themselves and on the streets. A French judge fell into this category of parent. He descended from a French immigrant family, was a widower, and had eleven daughters—

all of whom were unmarried. The living room was rather crowded, and the judge paid close attention to us all. There was limited room for alone time, so to speak. However, my friend among all these daughters was Felice. We discovered that it was possible to sneak in a moment of privacy when I first said goodbye to her father, and she walked me out to the front door. Here, there was an opportunity to explore our friendship further. It didn't last long, though, since the judge caught on to what was going on. He told Felice in no uncertain terms, 'he did not like these prolonged departures'.[1]

10

In the Spotlight

But it wasn't all classes and exams. Between each course there would sometimes be a large gap of time. At the start, before everything got going, I went through long periods of doing nothing. After two weeks or so of holiday, we got fed up, and wanted to crack on with our studies and flying. The first leave Harold and I got we spent in New York, a common venture the first time around. Everyone had read and heard so much about this metropolis, with all its skyscrapers, and the hectic pace of life on its streets. Of course we wanted to take a closer look at all this. We went all over Manhattan, soaking up everything around us. We took the elevator up to the top of the Empire State Building, from where we had a tremendous view of the entire city. We also went to Radio City and listened to all the programmes broadcasted from there. And we made a trip down to Harlem to take a look at the surroundings there. It was pretty filthy stuff; quite unsafe, too, especially at night.

In New York we wore our Norwegian uniforms, with the flag on one shoulder and 'NORWAY' written across the other. When we entered a restaurant and people saw that we were Norwegians, their hospitality reached new heights. They were so friendly and interested in us that we usually had trouble getting out of the restaurant again without being impolite. Everybody wanted to buy us drinks. If we so much as hinted at finishing our glasses, they just bought more. If we said we thought it was too much and that we wanted to pay for our own drinks, they wouldn't listen. They simply ignored our requests. So, when we finally did manage to get away and back out on the street, our moods had more than improved. We kept this up for seven days straight. Actually, we were both relieved to get back to Little Norway in the end. Perhaps a holiday really should be so intense that going back to work feels like a break in itself?

A letter that Gunnar Randers wrote to Finn in August 1942 still exists today. A friend of Eriksrud, Randers was employed by Yerkes Observatory in the USA from 1940 to 1941. He was several years Eriksrud's senior, and had most likely met Eriksrud at the boy scouts, where Randers was a leader before the war. Like Gunnar Høverstad, he too came from the Holmenkollen area in Oslo and made it to Little Norway. Randers became a member of the Technical Committee of the Norwegian High Command that year the letter was written. After the Second World War, he emerged as a principal figure within the Norwegian nuclear research community.

Dear Finn!

Thank you so much for your letter and the photo I received some time ago. I really appreciated it, and I hope you will let me keep it. You look very tight in that uniform—if I know you well, you will honour it too. As far as I could tell from Gunnar [Høverstad]'s letter, you have also been transferred from Toronto now. Is it flying or chopping wood these days? Or will you be a ferry pilot? It has to be a pretty good job I think, and well paid, too.

I am about to go to London, where I will most likely stay for the duration of the war. Engelke [not a Norwegian name, perhaps Dutch or a deviation of the German word 'Engel'] will join me, as far as I can presently tell. This week's work is done, so we're going back to Chicago to finish some personal business. Selling my car etc. Then I am on my way—maybe in a week, two weeks tops. I wish to keep in touch even once I have left—I will write to you and give you my address. By the way, you can always send a few words to me before I go [to Britain]. Write to Yerkes Observatory, Williams Bay, Wisconsin. I will get it when I arrive there.

On the king's birthday [2 August 1942] we went to a party at the embassy [in Washington D.C.]. Plenty of people there, about 200 I reckon. Most of them were only there for cocktails, but we and a few others got to stay for dinner as well. We had a jolly good time. Every Norwegian within miles came, as well as people from other embassies nearby.

We've also played a spot of tennis from time to time, but the climate is so useless you can't do anything—except walk around with a wet shirt. Say hello to your pals from me, and I will see you in England soon.

With best wishes from Engelke and myself—Gunnar Randers.

We got another holiday in the autumn of 1942. There were eight of us, and once more we went down to New York. At the same time that we were due to arrive in NYC, Paramount—the film company—was finishing up a film about the German occupation of Norway, and the Norwegians' passive and active

Above left: Harold Odman chopping wood in Canada (Gunnar Randers mentions chopping wood in his letter to Finn Eriksrud). The chopping was perhaps meant to ensure that pilots had enough firewood for the cold Canadian winter. (*Finn Eriksrud's collection*)

Above right: Finn Eriksrud taking a break from all the hard work. (*Finn Eriksrud's collection*)

Another photograph of Eriksrud on the same day of that Harold Odman chopped wood. (*Finn Eriksrud's collection*)

resistance. Paramount had beforehand asked Ole Reistad if he could send a few pilots down for the premiere, and so Reistad asked us if we wanted a return trip to New York and a few days' stay there, all expenses paid. This all fitted in nicely with our plans anyway, and we agreed. In New York, we were met by a representative of Paramount who took us to the best hotels in the city. On the night before the premiere, he gave us a little run-through about what we were supposed to do at the event. It turned out that the only thing expected of us was to stand to attention on the stage before the show started, while a Norwegian soldier sang the Norwegian and American national anthems.

The evening came, and everything went very smoothly. However, when we were done with our little task, the same representative approached us and asked if we wanted to join him at Madison Square Garden, where a bunch of actors and actresses were hosting a special show. We had heard plenty about this enormous building, and wanted to experience it first-hand, so we happily accepted his offer. We entered the venue literally through the back door, only to set eyes on something that resembled the Roman Coliseum, there being a great open space in the middle of it where they had, on this occasion, raised a podium. Thousands of people were seated around this, their seats raised upwards towards the roof.

The ballet from Radio City was on when we arrived. Once this was over and done with, the Paramount representative gestured to us to follow him. We thought we would finally be seated somewhere, but he led us through all the people and up onto that podium. I started to wonder how this little adventure would end. We lined up and looked around: the whole venue had fallen completely silent. It appeared that this was not on the official programme. To our great surprise, the American Paramount representative introduced us to the audience as eight Norwegian pilots arrived straight from Britain. He said we had been in the air during the Dieppe raid, and had shot down a total of twelve German bombers. We had absolutely no idea what to do in this situation. Stop him and tell people the truth? Perhaps there had been some kind of misunderstanding. The problem solved itself, however, as a massive roar of applause and cheers let rip. The only thing we could do was smile and take a bow. Afterwards, we asked him what the show was all about. He just shrugged it off and told us not to think of it. It was all about making the American people understand there was a war on, 'to make them war-minded,' as he put it. We had helped by bringing the people in that venue in direct contact with our war effort. The small fact that not one of us had so much as seen a German aircraft, let alone fired any guns at one in anger, was of little significance. *Mundus decipi vult*, he must have thought. *Let's deceive them.* Much later, when I was behind the barb-wired fence in Germany, I told a fellow Norwegian prisoner of this little experience. The story did not go down well with my friend. He had been shot down over Dieppe during the raid, and did not savour the fact that I had, almost at the same time, been in New York receiving all the applause for what he had been doing.

The film premiere and the unknown Norwegian Spitfire pilot

The film Eriksrud is talking about is the Paramount film *The Day Will Dawn*, or *Avengers*, as it was called in the USA. It premiered in New York on 24 November 1942.

The film is set in Norway at the outbreak of the war. British foreign correspondent Lockwood (Ralph Richardson), forced out of Norway by the Nazi invasion, is sent back to the occupied Scandinavian country by the War Office. Lockwood's assignment is to guide the RAF to a heavily camouflaged German U-boat base for sabotage purposes. Lockwood completes his mission with the help of patriotic Norwegian seaman Alstad (Finlay Currie), only to be arrested as a spy and sentenced to be shot. The final sequence of the film depicts the hero's attempt to escape back to England with Alstad's daughter Kari (Deborah Kerr), with whom he has fallen in love.

Eriksrud mentions a Norwegian pilot being shot down over Dieppe and taken prisoner on the same day as this premiere. The most likely candidate is Jan Staubo, a friend of his and a fellow prisoner of war in Bellaria, but it could also be Per Bergsland. They were both shot down over Dieppe during the Dieppe raid on 19 August 1942. Staubo survived the war and came back home to Norway in 1945; Bergsland participated in the Great Escape and was executed by the Gestapo in 1944. Another, less likely candidate is Thorstein Strand, who was shot down over Dieppe on 8 April 1943.

We didn't always travel to New York though, even if it was the place we were most drawn to. If we had time off during the winter, we would go where we could ski, even if it entailed a long journey. I spent my first winter in Canada travelling all the way to the Rocky Mountains, ignoring that I only had 36 hours of leave. I don't think I managed more than five hours of skiing that first winter. The next winter was a tad better in that respect, for Harold and I made it to the mountains close to Montreal. The landscape there reminded me a lot of Norway, so I felt at home and enjoyed it very much indeed. Harold had never really been skiing before. He was too young when he left Norway and in Portland they never had much snow. He made rapid progress though, and had a terrific time. He pinned all his honour to learning how to ski for being of Norwegian origin, he felt he needed to master this sport.

There was a ski-jumping hill not far from the hotel we stayed at. It was a medium-sized hill from which you could jump around 20 m. Many Canadians had never see anyone put skis on and literally fly down a hill before. Since I was from Norway and therefore born with skis on my feet, I was asked to show them how it was done. A number of years had passed since I had last ski-jumped, so I wasn't so sure I would do Norway and or the exercise any justice. No way out of it though—I had to do it, the Canadians insisted. I was cautious at first, but things went surprisingly well. However, there was a road that crossed the lower parts of the ski-jumping hill: I had to put weight on my skis in order not to fall down there. Because everything went so great at first, I quickly got arrogant and decided to make an extra jump where the road crossed the hill. It did not go down as well as I expected. I fell down heavily. The tip of my ski hit my eye hard, and within an hour my eye had turned a pretty shade of blue. The fact that it was New Year's Eve, and a big dinner and dancing had been planned in the evening, did not make matters any better. However, I have to admit that even with one blue eye, I was in high spirits.

We had plenty of fun when we were on leave. We hardly found time to think of those back in Norway, struggling with the occupation. Sometimes, though, we felt guilty because we had it so easy in Canada, or were reminded of how far from home we were when we red news of Norwegians being shot or sent to concentration camps. Our guilt subsided a little when we were sent to chop wood—at least we were doing something useful, even if we thought

Finn Eriksrud's class of pilots-to-be, Toronto 1941. Officers at the front, left to right; Capt. Bjørn Håkon Næss, Maj. Hans Grøn Lund, and Capt. John Magne Stene. Behind, from the left; Leif Eric Woodrow Hulthin, Reidar Døvle Moe, Bror Lars Burman Aarflot, Kjell Wilhelm Tvedt, Aksel Reidar Eikemo, Fridtjof Giørtz, Ole Tobias Mehn-Andersen, Harald Jensen, Harold Odman, Niels Stockleth Darre Eckhoff, Andreas Hofgaard Wyller, Carl Thorleif Johnsen, Rolf Leithe, Thore Stensrud, and Finn Eriksrud.

it a bit odd to make it all the way to Canada only to chop wood. As I have mentioned before, when at the end of one course we had to wait a long time for the next, we would get restless and wish for active duty as soon as possible. Harold got so impatient he gave up flying bombers altogether, and asked to be transferred to fighters instead. He got his wish. By the time he got his fighter wings, we bomber boys were also done with our courses, so he didn't really get to participate in the war any faster than the rest of us.

Finally, on 6 January 1943 we all left New York harbour with a couple of thousand American officers and soldiers. The ship was called the '*Queen Elizabeth*', and it took us from New York to Glasgow. She was completely full, so the best thing we could do was stay in our bunks. At least no one stepped on you if you were lucky enough to get the top bunk. On the first day or so we were escorted by ships and aircraft, but for the remainder of the journey, we steamed across the Atlantic on our own. It took no more than four days to reach Glasgow, and without any sort of trouble at all.

11

The Fate of Harold Odman

On the fourth and final day of our crossing we were met by English aircraft. They escorted us up the Firth of Clyde. The anchor came down in the river outside Greenock. It took a while before everyone disembarked in Glasgow because the *Queen Elizabeth* could not get into the harbour. By the evening we had all been packed off to London by train. Finally, I was going to see the war for the first time. But thick curtains on board the train hindered any sort of view of the outside—it was pitch black.

Both Harold and I were exhilarated at arriving in England and had high hopes of making it to an operational squadron. Harold was a fighter pilot, and was quickly sent to a fighter station upon arriving in London. Bomber pilots, myself included, had to wait an entire month in the nation's proud capitol. In the meantime, I got a job on the staff of the Norwegian Air Force Administration. I was tasked with writing birthday cards and greetings to Air Force personnel.

Harold Odman

Harold Odman's career as a fighter pilot was to be short-lived. He joined No. 332 Squadron based at North Weald, Essex, on 13 April 1943 and became fully operational the month after, flying a Spitfire Vb (even though the squadron was mostly equipped with Spitfire IX at this time). He was credited with probably shooting down a Focke-Wulf Fw 190 on 17 June, and damaging another on the same day. On 15 July 1943, Odman participated in Rodeo 245 with both the Norwegian Spitfire squadrons (No. 331 and No. 332) led by acting wing commander Rolf Arne Berg. When the squadron reached the Abbeville area, they turned north towards St. Omer. Odman was seen straggling, and did not respond to orders over the radio to keep in formation. He never replied and was seen to fall behind, which might indicate that his oxygen was not working, or he had forgotten to turn it on. No one saw him crash—he simply disappeared from the formation.

Fellow No. 332 Squadron pilot Rolf M. Kolling was one of Odman's best friends. He especially remembered an eerie episode just a few days prior to Odman's disappearance. Odman had told Kolling to visit him in his room at the base, where Kolling saw that he had organised all of his belongings. He showed Kolling photos of his fiancé in Oregon, as well as a nice small leather oval suitcase. Out of the blue, Odman told Kolling that he could have it when he didn't return, and gave him a photo of his fiancé. He kept pointing to things that Kolling would get the day he died, as well as the addresses of several contacts in Canada whom he should notify of the death. According to Kolling, all pilots knew that their belongings would be shared if one were not to return, but Harold Odman's meticulous planning left him disconcerted. It seemed as though Odman knew he would not make it through the war.

Odman was later found by the Germans in France, and buried in a grave-yard in Hesdin. His remains were brought home to Orkanger in Trøndelag, after the war. His father did not learn of his son's death until October 1945.

After a month on birthday card duty, I was finally sent to an airfield close to the Bristol Channel. I had to got used to flying in England and adapted to the situation at hand. There was a gigantic difference between flying in Canada

Norwegian-American Harold Odman, one of Eriksrud's best friends in Canada.

and flying in England. In Canada, if we came across a railroad or a road, there could be little doubt as to which it was. In England, it was a whole other story: there were so many railroads and roads crossing each other that getting on top of things seemed hopeless.

Every time I got lost and knew I was about to make a big mess of things, I set course for the Bristol Channel, the only landmark I could easily spot. Once above it, I would start my navigation all over again. Compared to Canada, there were also an awful lot more aircraft flying around in England, so I had to constantly be on the alert. Bomber activity over Germany was very busy in those days, and I could often spot fighter and bomber formations heading east. Later in the afternoon I would see them returning, their formations split and many of them full of gaping holes left by lost bombers. More often than not, bombers came back alone and with one or two engines out of action. Conversely, German activity over England was minimal, and during the day time stopped altogether. Those who dared to cross the Channel did so at night, and usually solo. They fled back to Europe so quickly that it was hard to chase them down.

If flying around England during the day time was a different experience, night flying there was even more so. It was actually easier to find my way when it was dark. There were always things to distract me during the daytime. At night, I didn't see anything at all and felt this to be in my favour. If I flew above 1,600 feet, I couldn't even see the lights from the airfield I was circling. I liked having the pundit beacons around (a type of navigational lighthouse on the ground). The British moved them around from time to time though. If I got lost, I usually flew over to the nearest pundit beacon and circled it while emitting my call signal. The people stationed at the pundit beacon would then turn on a bright light and direct it towards the nearest airfield. The only thing I had to do was to fly on this course. Further down another pundit beacon would be lit, and so on. When I finally came into the airfield, they would light several points to create a cone shape straight over the airfield. All I had to do then was land. I also received great help from something the English called 'occults'. Unlike pundit beacons, occults were stationed in one of three positions. The reason the occults changed positions was that the Germans might use them to fix a position over England at night.

Before I went up, I was always told what kind of letters the different occults were sending up, and in which of these three positions they would be that night. Whenever I saw an occult, I knew my position beyond a doubt.

'Darky' was a call signal often used when someone lost wanted help from the ground at night. We also identified ourselves by giving out information about what squadron we belonged to, and the squadron code of our aircraft. The name of the squadron was always in code. These were changed often so that the Germans couldn't keep up on how the different squadrons operated.

The names themselves are meaningless. My squadron was called 'Ceader' for some time. I doubt you will find that in any dictionary.

If I sent out the call signal 'Larky', I would get a response from the nearest airfield and they would then give me the information I requested. If I wanted to know my position, they would tell me. If I wanted to land at the nearest airfield, I was given the correct course for it. I also followed a course to land on a radio beam.

So far, I had only been flying the training type of aircraft. I was very impatient to fly a real warbird, though. We had all been given a very detailed education, that's for sure. Many of us sometimes thought it was a bit over the top. But this airfield by the Bristol Channel was the last stop before joining an operational squadron—the last polish, so to speak, of my skills as a pilot. The other Norwegians were sent to a squadron in the middle of England, while I was sent up to Scotland. It was from here that the Norwegians were launching operations over the Norwegian coast.

The two Norwegian Air Forces

Up until 1944, the Norwegian Air Force was split into two separate services: one military—the Army Air Force—and one naval—the Navy Air Force.

No. 330 Squadron (of the Navy Air Force) was the first of its kind to be established in Iceland, in the spring of '41, with Northrop N-3PBs. Its task consisted of flying recce missions over the North Atlantic. The squadron was later furnished with Consolidated Catalinas. In 1943, it received Short Sunderlands and moved its operations to Scotland for the remainder of the war.

Two fighter squadrons (of the Army Air Force) were established in June 1941—No. 331 Squadron—and January 1942—No. 332 Squadron. No. 331 Squadron began its operations at Skeabrae, in the Orkneys, before being sent to North Weald in May 1942. No. 332 Squadron operated from Catterick, in Yorkshire, before being sent to North Weald in June 1942. The Norwegians operated as part of the North Weald Wing (later named 132 Wing) until the end of the war. They remained at North Weald until they moved to Bognor Regis shortly before the invasion of Europe in 1944. After operating on the continent with the RAF's Second Tactical Air Force, they returned to North Weald shortly before VE day. The two squadrons then left for Norway with their Spitfires.

A further naval squadron was established in February 1942 (No. 333 Squadron). Its task consisted of recce sorties over the coast of Norway, as well as flying in and withdrawing secret agents using Catalinas. A B-Flight was established in the spring of 1943 at Leuchars, Scotland, with de Havilland Mosquitos also flying recce sorties over the Norwegian coastline. It was this flight that Finn Eriksrud would join as a Navy pilot.

On 10 November 1944, the Army Air Force and the Navy Air Force were merged to form the Royal Norwegian Air Force.

The Norwegian Navy had a flight of Catalinas based at Woodhaven, just north of Dundee. Woodhaven was under the control of Leuchars, where a new flight of Mosquitos were to be formed. This was where I was going. I arrived at Leuchars in the middle of April 1943. However, no Mosquitos had arrived yet, although two English Beaufighter squadrons were operating from the airfield. It was initially decided that we would have a flight of Mosquitos, not a squadron, and six of these machines arrived fourteen days after my own arrival. We immediately started training on the Mosquitos so we could get going with operations as soon as possible. Training was interesting indeed: firstly, because these were the aircraft we would be using on real operations of war, and secondly, because it would not be long now before we would be flying these sorties.

The Mosquito was a great aircraft. It had only been operational since relatively recently. Everyone who flew them was thrilled. They were heavily armed, too—four machine guns mounted on the nose, and slightly further down, four 20-mm cannons. The Mosquitos could also carry 2,000-kg bombs, but we used that space for an extra fuel tank to keep us flying longer. We had no weapons further back, so to get away from an attack from the rear, we had to rely on our speed—and what a speed it was. We were easily up there with the fastest German fighters.

The Mossie (a popular nickname for the type) had a crew of two—the pilot and the navigator. They had better be friends, because space was limited at best. It was essential that they worked well together: even when we were out just

---

Norwegian Mosquitos

The Mosquitos which arrived shortly after Finn Eriksrud's arrival at Leuchars were of the F Mk. II type. They were not designed to accommodate any load under their wings. Later on, in September 1943, the flight also got hold of the FB Mk. VI, a fighter bomber version with the possibility of carrying weapons and drop tanks from under its wings.

The Mk. II Mossies were all camouflaged in a standard scheme from the de Havilland factory—medium sea-grey and dark green. The letters were a dull red, and there were B-type roundels on the upper part of the wings—they had no roundel on the undersides. The Norwegians quickly painted the Norwegian flag on either side of the nose. The flight received a total of eight Mk. IIs in this first period at Leuchars. Its last Mk II was lost on 30 April 1944.

No. 333 Squadron's first Mosquitos: Serial DZ744 with letter G and 3G; Serial DZ700 with letter H; Serial DZ752 with letter E; Serial DZ754 with letter F; Serial DZ745 with letter D and J; Serial DZ711 with letter L; Serial DZ705 with letter E; and Serial DD690 with letter F. All of them arrived between 23 April 1943 and 26 July 1943.

A Norwegian Mosquito being worked on. Notice the neatly painted flag under the cockpit. (*Forsvarsmuseet*)

Another Mosquito being worked on. (*Forsvarsmuseet*)

practising shooting at ground targets, for example, the navigator was there. I was lucky and got a short navigator, so there was some space to spare between us. His name was Erling Johanssen and he came from Kristiansand, Norway. He left Norway in 1939 for a spell as a sailor. When France capitulated in 1940, the ship he was on and her entire crew was put under arrest in Bona, North Africa. They were there for a whole ten months. Erling got sick of it, though, and decided to escape. With a few others they decided to get hold of a boat and row over the Mediterranean. Many adventures later, they reached Spain. From there they boarded a Spanish fishing boat to Gibraltar, and from there were sent to England, where Erling volunteered for the Norwegian Air Force. He took a radiotelegraphy course, and also a navigation course. It was his job to be both navigator and telegraphist. For a good month we flew and trained together, becoming better acquainted. We came to collaborate well and trust each other to the fullest.

A slightly blurred and poor-quality photograph of Johanssen in his uniform. (*Erling Johanssen's collection*)

Erling Victor Johanssen

Erling Johanssen came from Kristiansand, in southernmost Norway. He was the grandson of one of the founders of Fædrelandsvennen, the local newspaper. Johanssen finished his artium degree and joined the Norwegian shipping company Hansen-Tangen. He was hired aboard the ship M/T *Regina*, which on his third trip in 1940—bringing oil from USA to Europe—was taken into custody by the French and then interned in Oran, Algeria. The British gave the commander of the French forces in North-Africa an ultimatum: surrender the ships or face an attack. The admiral declined, and the British launched an offensive in which the French lost about 2,000 men, and after which most of the French fleet returned to France. Johanssen's ship was sent to Bone, still remaining in Algeria. As Finn wrote in his book, he decided to escape—by mixing sleeping tablets he had got from a French doctor into some wine and giving it to the crew. He made his getaway, together with Per Thulin and five others from the neighbouring ship *Varanger*, in a stolen life-boat. They endured thirteen days at sea before arriving at Cartagena in Spain. They then made it to Gibraltar aboard a Spanish cargo ship. Johanssen reported for duty with the Norwegian forces, but could not become a pilot on account of his eye vision. He was to become a navigator instead, and joined Finn Eriksrud as such at No. 333 Squadron in 1943.

12

The Deadly Norwegian Coast

I was at last ready to start operations on the Norwegian coast in June 1943. I had been in training in the Royal Air Force for two whole years. It was with great anticipation that I had awaited that first trip to Norway in a Mosquito.

Finn Eriksrud's first sorties over the Norwegian coastline

According to No. 333 Squadron's ORB, Eriksrud did not fly to Norway until 2 July 1943. It is possible that his first patrol was not listed, but not very likely. Finn Eriksrud's first visit to the Norwegian coast is recorded to have taken place at mid-day, and not in the morning, as he writes below. He took off from Leuchars with his navigator Erling Johanssen at 10.10 a.m., and landed at 2.12 p.m., having completed a four-hour-long recce in the area between Sulen, Vilnesfjord, Skjongfjord, and Rikefjord (north of Bergen, and heading northwards). Eriksrud and Johanssen spotted a ship of approximately 4,500 to 5,000 tonnes halfway through the recce, and reported this back to base. The patrol continued at 2,000 feet over Bremanger, Vågsø, Stadtlandet, Sande, and up to Ålesund. While this recce may be the one he recounts below, it is equally possible that Finn confusedly injected elements of other patrols over Norway into this narrative.

Further on, the first registered sortie to Norway undertaken by No. 333 Squadron was flown on 27 May 1943 by flight commander Håkon Offerdahl and his navigator Quartermaster A. Poulsen. This was an early morning patrol. They arrived back at Leuchars at around 9 a.m. having taken off three hours earlier.

For this first trip, we (my navigator and I) were awakened in the middle of the night. Our sortie would take place at dawn. We were served a hearty breakfast of bacon and eggs, after which we went to the Ops room, the centre of any airfield. The chaps who had worked in the Ops room knew all about our own and enemy aircraft operating over the North Sea or along the Norwegian coastline. The Ops room was also in contact with 18 Group in Edinburgh,

All set for Norway! Finn Eriksrud shily smiles for the cameraman, most likely in Scotland in 1943. (*Tor Idar Larsen's collection*)

whose headquarters controlled several local airfields, and from whom flight orders were sent. The first thing we saw when we came into the Ops room was a large map of Scotland, the North Sea, and Norway, painted across a large wall. There was a red line strung out from Leuchars over the ocean to Bergen, then onwards to Ålesund and back again to Leuchars. There were also several areas painted dark by the coastline, within which there were yellow pins. These were allied submarines. If we spotted submarines inside these marked fields we were not to attack. There were also two large black areas marked just by the entrance to the Sognefjord, where two German submarines had been observed the day before. We could attack those as much as we wanted. Submarines and aircraft were all that what we were allowed to fire upon: we were to stay away from ships and flak batteries, only send back messages of their position and let others take care of them. The mainland German positions were marked with red pins, beside which stood information about the number of cannons and their calibre. Likewise, German-controlled airfields were marked with blue pins and their type of aircraft and numerical strength provided.

An intelligence officer approached Erling and me, and explained that the red line on the map was our route. Our task consisted of patrolling the distance from Bergen to Ålesund on the west coast of Norway. Whether we wanted to fly north–south or south–north was up to us—we usually chose to fly towards Bergen first thereafter, because there was a German fighter airfield there and we figured we could come at it with an element of surprise. We could be well on our way north before they had time to react, which would give us the advantage of a head start on German fighters trying to chase us down, rather than having to meet them head on. With the Mosquitos' great speed at our disposal, we figured we could keep the fighters at a safe distance. If we flew the opposite way, from north to south, we figured we would risk flying towards the Germans, which we thought a poor choice. There was no point in us getting into a dogfight with two or more machines from the German opposition. They could manoeuvre much better than us, and were superior in most aspects, with the exception of speed. It was for the best to keep away from them. Erling plotted in the course on the map, measured the distances, and calculated our time of arrival over the Norwegian coastline. He also calculated our estimated time of arrival back at Leuchars. The intelligence officer pointed to the map and gave us information about German fighters stationed along the coastline: their most likely method of patrol over the area, where the flak batteries were placed, and how many of them each location had. We were also warned about those places where electricity cables could be hazardous to our flying—we were to fly low for the entire duration of our sortie so that the German radar would have a hard time picking us up. The radar could spot us if we were about 200 km away, and did not fly higher than about 3,000 feet. If we stayed lower we would not be detected, and at only a few feet above sea level, the Germans would not detect us until we were within 50 km of the coast. This, of course, was due to the shape of the Earth, which by all means turned out not to be far from the truth. One day, we were on our return leg and had flown extra low; Erling was near the mark when he commented that, 'when we left the instrument showed our speed in miles, but it got so full of salt and sea water that it self-converted to indicate knots instead'.

Before take-off we each received a little waterproof box. This contained a small compass, a hacksaw, 100 Nok in cash, and a map of Norway. This was all given to us in case we were shot down, with the help of which our chances of getting back to England either by sea or crossing into Sweden (which was more likely). We also carried signal pistols in case we needed to alert any British ships or aircraft of our identity. It was decided that, at certain points in the day, it was necessary to shoot those flares to avoid being shot at by our own side. One day the colour might be yellow, and on another it might well change to something else.

In the radio room we got the right codes and our signal name, which was valid for the time we would be out flying. Then we walked over to the met office where large weather maps were spread out on a table. The meteorologist plucked the right one of the bunch and pointed to certain places on the map.

He explained to us what kind of weather we would be expecting out in the North Sea and over the Norwegian coast. Next we found our way over to the Ops room, where we got a little box containing chocolate, a few caramels, raisins, and a can of orange juice. To make sure we didn't miss out, we ate everything before we took off anyway, at times before we had even stepped into the cockpit.

It was still dark when we came out of the Ops room on that first night of operations over Norway. The weather was brilliantly clear, the sky completely clear of clouds. It was all set to go very well for us, the patrol would certainly benefit from such weather. Then we walked down to the hangars. The boys there were already in full swing working on the Mosquito. They had worked through the night to get it ready. While we had been in briefing, they had pushed it out of the hangar, filled it up with fuel and ammunition, and ran up the engines. Reistad sure was right when he said every man was equally important for our cause. Results indeed depended on every one of us doing our job well—no matter what it was, it was extremely important. What would we have done without the boys on the ground? They regularly had to stay on duty from early morning to very late at night, making sure our precious Mossies were in peak working condition. The ground crew's labour yielded little excitement or drama, and gave no chance of recognition, or promotion, for that matter. But their work was full of serious responsibility, and they knew it. They also knew that we the pilots trusted them with our lives, and that our fate was in their hands.

Once the Mosquito was cleared by the ground crew, Erling and I got into our Mae Wests and parachutes. We climbed aboard and settled inside the small cockpit. I remember the engines starting up on the first try, and that all the instruments worked like those of a Mosquito primed and ready. I gave the engines a bit of a burst, and we followed the airfield lights towards the end runway. A couple of minutes later, we were ready for take-off. A green light from the tower. One last check of the gages, to which Erling gave a reassuring nod of approval. I opened the throttle and off we went for our first Norwegian sortie. A quick circle over Leuchars while Erling gave me the correct course for Bergen. It was finally on.

From past to present
At this point in the original book, Finn's narrative shifts to the present tense. We decided to follow suit in the translation, to make as little change as possible to his style of writing in 1945. He stuck with the present tense until the end of this patrol story.

Behind us, we see the silhouettes of the Scottish mountains. The first rays of sunlight catch our Mosquito as we cross the Scottish coastline. The magnificent view of Great Britain disappears quickly and the North Sea surrounds us on all sides. We leave miles and miles behind us over the open sea. The speed shows 420 kph. At this rate, we expect to reach the Norwegian coastline within the hour, staying at 900 feet above sea level.

With 6 miles to go we lower ourselves to sea level. As low as we can possibly get. I push the throttle forward and the speed increases quickly to 470 kph. It's all about coming in unnoticed by the Germans. If they find out we are in the area, they will scramble fighters to meet us.

I notice the wind has changed a little. It is now coming from the north, so Erling calculates a new course and time of our arrival at the coast. Outside the day has dawned, and we are flying in clear sunlight. For Erling, it's especially important that we approach the coast at the right place and at the right time. It's a matter of honour for him to do this correctly. Yet neither of us has ever been to the western coast of Norway before! We only know it from photographs we studied in detail at Leuchars after we arrived in April.

The time Erling had given me for our arrival at the enemy coast comes up, and we expect to see land at any minute. It's a peculiar feeling to come back to Norway after two and a half years of separation. Within minutes I will see it again, but only for a short while. I catch myself speculating how long it will be until we can stop having to illicitly return to our own country, flying up and down our coast like a bunch of criminals. I think about all those people down there, having a terrible time living under German occupation. How long will it all last?

My thoughts are interrupted by Erling. He touches my shoulder gently and points to starboard. I quickly spot what he's pointing to—the Norwegian coastline, a small, thin line of land in the sea gradually widening out as we approach it. The Norwegian national anthem starts running in my head. Its composer certainly made some good points in his lyrics.

We are both so excited to see Norway that we forget to find out where we are exactly. We're just sitting there, staring at our home country. Everything is so quiet and calm, and there is no sign of that a war is going on. We fly past a fishing boat with a big Norwegian flag flapping in the wind. I waggle the Mosquitos wings so the fisherman will understand that his fellow countrymen are coming back home, if only for a short visit. Further up the coast we thunder over a small rowing boat, close to the shoreline. When he discovers the Mosquito he gets up and starts waving like mad. It's a miracle the small boat doesn't capsize. I give in to temptation and circle the boat once, hoping he will see the Norwegian flag we have painted below the cockpit window. This is bloody good fun!

I push the Mossie low and fast over the coastline. Sometimes we spot small, white houses. The people out here don't require much more than being left alone to their work. It's a harsh environment this close to the cold North Sea.

Reaching the Norwegian coastline. Many of Eriksrud's sorties must have looked something like this, approaching Norway at a low angle and full speed. (*Forsvarsmuseet*)

For generations they've plied the same trade, now frequently disturbed by low-flying aircraft storming over their houses and making such a racket.

Suddenly we see two rows of red and green lights fast approaching us. Flak! So, there is a war on after all. We had both forgotten all about it for a moment. It's not as peaceful as it first appeared. There doesn't seem to be much love for us here, either, and we come to the brutal realisation that we're not welcome.

In order not to become a sitting duck for German gunners I change course and altitude. I keep doing this until we're out of their artillery's reach. I suspect only expertly trained gunners could shoot us down at the speed we're going at. We follow the coast northwards. We pass the Sognefjord (north of Bergen, Norway's longest fjord) on our left side. Those submarines we saw on the map before take-off are long gone, we see no sign of them. Further on we pass Atleøen, and the small town of Florø. We spot nothing of interest there. The Stad peninsula comes into view shortly after the dead town that was Florø. We immediately spot smoke rising up close to the tall mountains—a German convoy, moving north. We change course directly towards it, and Erling gets his camera ready. If he snaps a few good ones, the various ships may be recognised by experts when we arrive back at Leuchars. We stare with focused eyes at the German ships. The convoy consists of four cargo ships, about 5,000 to 6,000 tonnes each. In the middle there's a tanker, maybe 8,000 tonnes. Their escort consists of a destroyer and four smaller naval vessels that look like whaling ships.

One of the ships shoots off a red flare. We wonder about it for a second, but the Germans' next move leaves us in no doubt. They fire everything they've got at us. From what we can see, all of it ends up in the sea behind us. I break out in a sweat and feel uncomfortable. Erling is taking notes as fast as he can. Size of the convoy, position, speed, course, its escort, and at what time all of this happens. As soon as we can we will report this back to Leuchars. Erling gives me a short nod. He got everything he wanted. I have no hesitation in getting out of here as quickly as possible. The gunners are closing in on us, and fast. We move out of range. Safe once more.

We fly around the peninsula and the coast takes us further east. Then we head north again. We spot more fishing boats and a few other small boats as well. Nothing of importance for our patrol. We then fly between Sula and Yksnøen in order to get on the east side of the town of Ålesund. We hope that the Germans won't be expecting us there, for the most predictable offensive point of entry would be the harbour area, from the west side, as is confirmed when we come in here a week later. They didn't get us then either, but it was a close call. On this sortie though, we surprise them and get several decent photos of the town and harbour. Long after we leave them behind, they start to fire at us. They are wasting their time, for we are far out of range.

By now, we're finished with our patrol, and the only thing left to fear are German fighters from Gossen, located south of Kristiansund. They can intercept us on our way back. We're both keeping an eye out for those dangerous Focke Wulf Fw 190 fighters. Erling stares at our rear and starboard flank. I'm looking ahead and to our port side. Suddenly I hear the words I dread the most: 'Four fighters behind us!'

Gossen Airfield

Gossen Airfield was built by the Germans in 1943 on Aukra Island, about 33 miles north of Ålesund. The runway is 1,200 m long and consists of wood-work rather than asphalt. It was an important strategic airfield for the Germans, bombed several times by the Allies during the war. After hostilities ended, Gossen became a civilian airfield and hosted other activities in the air—it still does today, and is also simply known as Aukra Airfield. There has more recently been talk of upgrading the airfield in correlation with the region's growing industry.

I increase the speed of our Mosquito to the absolute maximum. We shall soon find out if they can catch up, or if we can keep them at a distance. There is no immediate danger. Yet. They can't fire at us from this range and expect to hit us. They would at least have to wait until the 600-m mark to get in a few shots at us. Yet again, I get that strange sensation in my gut and I sweat like a pig. There are no clouds about so we just have to keep them at a safe distance, relying on our speed. I take comfort in words from Erling that I've heard before; how the Germans don't want to venture very far out from the coastline. By this time I expect them to turn back, considering how far out we are from the mainland. But they don't seem to be turning back yet. I tensely wait for Erling's next reassurance. He surely will tell me if they are catching up, and the wait for his next report is nerve-wracking. I give up the wait and turn my head for just a fraction of a second to look for the fighters. They are closer. From what I can tell, they have halved the distance between us since the last time I looked. More sweating, more nerves.

A couple of minutes more and they finally give up and head back to Norway. They most likely realised they could not catch us in time. I feel extremely relieved when the last one disappears into the horizon behind us. If they had caught up with us, or managed to sneak further in on us before Erling had spotted them, I don't know what would have happened, only that it wouldn't have been pretty. I think it's more than likely we would have succumbed to those four Focke Wulf Fw 190s. Perhaps we might have stood a fighting chance if there had been only two of them. But not four. Back in Scotland we had been training with English fighters, learning how to deal with these situations, and how to manoeuvre in the correct way. We were to find out that two fighters on our tail were the absolute limit of what we could handle.

I gradually decrease the speed again, and climb the Mossie to a higher altitude so our signals will be stronger and received by Leuchars. Erling gets a connection at once, and sends out a report about the German convoy we spotted. This message is then sent to the Ops room at Leuchars where the intelligence officer goes through it in order to decide if any ships in the convoy are valuable enough to send the Beaufighters in. The tanker we saw should be enough to warrant an attack, we are quite sure. The Beaufighters have been on stand by while we've been out, just in case we spotted something of interest.

Our report has done the trick. We see the Beaufighters pass beneath us on their way to the convoy in Norway. Twelve of them in total. Good luck to them, they will need it.

Norwegian coastal vessels were frequently preyed on by allied fighters and bombers. We had strict orders not to attack any boats weighing in under 1,000 tonnes if they were not part of a convoy. We did, however, have orders to attack them if they fired at us first. The Norwegians flying over the coastline knew the score and stayed away from them. But the British and the Canadians, having only seen these ships in photographs, were more curious. So, when they spotted them they went in for a closer look. If there were Germans on board, they would interpret their curiosity as an attack and start firing. The British would then naturally conclude that the ship was German and fight back. I think this a reasonable explanation of why so many coastal ships were lost during the war.

Back to our mission: we land with all our limbs intact. We leave our Mosquito in the capable hands of our ground crew. They will inspect it and make it ready for another patrol. Erling and I go to the Ops room again to give a report of what we've seen. We also give them our photographs. The met officer wants to know if his weather map corresponds to the actual weather on the other side of the North Sea. For the rest of the day, we're off duty. We can do whatever want, but we so are tired we catch some sleep before we do anything else.

Finn Eriksrud and Erling Johanssen's first victory

Finn must have had his reasons for not mentioning his victories in his book. One can only speculate as to what they were. Finn scored his first victory on only his third sortie, on 9 July 1943. Johanssen and he took off in Mosquito DZ705 E at 4.24 p.m. for a weather and shipping recce over Norway. Somewhere along the coastline, in poor weather, they spotted a Junkers Ju 88. Eriksrud approached it from behind, going in for an attack. They were puzzled to observe that the enemy aircraft fired a red star cartridge, followed by another just five seconds later. The Mosquito quickly caught up with the enemy, and Finn opened fire with the Mossie's cannons. Hits were observed all along the Ju 88's fuselage, and its port engine rapidly caught fire. The Norwegians then passed the German aircraft, and Johanssen turned around in his chair to see the enemy go down in flames and crash into the sea. Neither of the two boys had seen any return fire from the German bomber, which, combined with the odd cartridges it had initially fired, led them to believe that the Germans had mistaken them for friends, not recognising the Mosquito as an enemy aircraft.

A case of mistaken identity: it was in fact a Focke Wulf Fw 85 Weihe that the crew of the Mosquito had attacked in December 1943, their last victory in the war. (*Heinz Feldner's collection*)

Eriksrud and Johanssen arrived safely back at Leuchars at 7.17 p.m.

Unbeknown to the two Norwegians at the time, they too had a case of mistaken identity on their hands. According to researchers Kjetil Korsnes and Bengt Stangvik, they shot down a Focke Wulf Fw 58 on 9 July, and not a Ju 88. This was a sea-rescue aircraft operating from Herdla Airfield and bound for Lade, not far from Trondheim. There has been some discussion since about whether this Fw 58 was armed or not. It did have the capacity to carry two 7.92-mm MG-15 machine guns. In any case, Finn and Erling had just made their first kill.

13

B-Flight's Losses

Being a pilot is in my opinion the best and most comfortable job you could have during a war. We had a permanent base, always had a roof over our heads, a good bed, and basically all those necessities one could have in a modern society. Before we went on our patrols, we always got a hot meal served in peaceful surroundings. Everything seemed to be adjusted to our needs. We had a warm aircraft to sit in, and if we did end up in a dogfight, all the action happened from a distance. We didn't have to watch our enemies suffer, and we never really saw any blood either. We were never ordered to fix a bayonet and aim for someone's gut. I'm also not sure whether you could get a bomber pilot to continue doing his job for extended periods if he were to witness all the devastation he caused on the ground. After we had landed after a sortie, we were done for the day. We could get a hot bath if we wanted to, and if we felt tired we could take a nap without being awakened by the thunder of cannons or grenades falling on top of us. However, there were situations where I wished I had never set foot in an aircraft at all. Just be some normal ground trooper instead, dug in in some fox hole somewhere. I truly wished that was the case the time that Erling and I were out flying a navigational training sortie over the North Sea. The weather was terrible, with strong winds and rain.

We had flown for two hours when I discovered that we had spent the last half hour flying on the wrong course. I was flying a 360-degree course instead of 180, and because of me we were well on our way to Svalbard Island. The only thing we could do was to keep the same course until Erling had calculated just about where we were and then set a new course for land again. In this case, that land would have to be the Shetland Islands. Erling made his calculations, but the estimated time at which we would see the Shetlands came and went. We didn't see a thing. Just darkness. We had tried to reach them by radio, but there was not a sound to be heard. We started to wonder whether we had flown past the Shetlands completely, and were heading out into the

A busy day for the Norwegians at Leuchars. (*Forsvarsmuseet*)

Atlantic. However, Lady Luck was on our side that day. Half an hour later we saw land. We had no idea where we were, but we were convinced it could not be the Shetlands. It was still dark when we landed. We turned off the engines and got out of the Mossie. It turned out we had landed on an airfield just at the northern tip of Scotland, because, as we later discovered, the northern winds had increased significantly while we had been out flying, unbeknownst to us. Erling had calculated the course to the Shetlands using the same wind speed he had been given before take-off, and with that strong wind blowing against our Mosquito, we had drifted way out of course. We had flown high up for the duration of this hairy trip, so that the beacons could get a fix on our location, which they did in earnest. Apparently, we had caused quite a stir in the Ops room when they discovered we were flying north instead of south. They had called out to us over the radio but got no reply from us; they had given us the right courses for home, but we didn't hear a thing. A comfort, if any, in all of this was that they knew within a decent margin of error where we would have ended up if we had been forced to ditch in the sea. If they managed to find us it would be a different matter altogether. A small dinghy floating in the North Sea in bad weather would be hard to spot indeed.

Leuchars was a very pleasant airfield. It was built before the war, so we lived in solid houses where everything was well organised, in my point of view. The airfields knocked together during the war were primitive in comparison.

They were also very cold in the winter, and not altogether pleasant to live in. Such was the state of affairs in the Shetlands, where we would later stay for a while. Most of the airfields had organised entertainment for us to enjoy: movies were shown on the big screen several times a week, and at least once a week dances were held. There were women on all airfields in Britain. They did office work, for example, and also radio communication in case anyone flying needed instructions; they worked in the kitchens, too, and in the mess. They were not confined to just these tasks, though: several worked as mechanics, and in the hangars. They did a top job. More than often, lorries arrived at the airfield driven by a tiny female inside. I did get used to them working in the kitchen and driving cars and lorries, but having them carry out inspections on my Mossie before patrols was harder to grow accustomed to. It did make life at the airfield a much brighter affair, though. It was very pleasant to have some female company, rather than just being surrounded by men.

In the summer of 1943, two of our Mosquitos were sent up to Sumburgh, just at the southern tip of the Shetlands. They were taken there by two crew, and I was among them. We enjoyed life in the north. Firstly, we were very close to the Norwegian coastline: it only took 45 minutes to reach Bergen. And we could also do patrols much further north than had we been flying out from Leuchars. It was a quiet life up there, there wasn't that much to do in our spare time.

We spent many hours in Lerwick visiting the crews of a few Norwegian torpedo-boats stationed there. Those chaps had many interesting stories to tell from their sorties in Norway.

I still remember one particular sortie they told us about. There was a terrible storm that day, and they had no way of getting back home to Lerwick. The only thing they could do until the storm calmed down was stay put. They camouflaged their vessel as well as could be done in a Norwegian fjord, and ended up staying there for a week. Twice a day a German patrol boat came by them, and it never detected their presence. The guys had also sunk many German ships and shot down several aircraft. One time, we in our Mossie passed two such boats on our way back to Scotland. We kept at a distance from them, as we had seen their boats up close and they were armed to the teeth. The boys on board were easy on the trigger, too, and didn't know much about aircraft recognition. A week later, we met the guys once again, and they told us that the alarm had gone off on their boat. They had spotted us, but had thankfully recognised our Mossie.

Alongside us at Sumburgh was a Beaufighter squadron armed with torpedoes, and another squadron equipped with rockets. Each of those aircraft had four of these big projectiles mounted on each wing. When they fired off all together, the damage was considerable. The negative side was of course that, once everything had been fired off, they had to go back and load up again.

We kept up our routine patrols over the coastline of Norway, and our collaboration with the Beaufighters improved as time went by. To begin with, they couldn't always spot those convoys we reported back on, though this was pretty rare. They gradually learnt to find them on the spot.

My excitement about the sorties to Norway had begun to dissipate by high summer in 1943. If I knew in the afternoon that I would be flying the next day, I didn't sleep very well. I stayed awake for most of the night thinking about our tactics for the upcoming task; where to approach the coastline so we would surprise the Germans; and how to avoid any route we had been on before. We had to accept the fact that the Germans moved their flak batteries around from time to time. So if we flew over one route one day and this was uneventful, we couldn't count on it being so peaceful the next time around. I guess the constant fear of being shot down and the mental strain of flying these patrols had started to kick in.

It was navigator Jan Heide and pilot Knut Skavhaugen who came with me and Erling to Sumburgh. Knut knew the coastline well, from civilian flying there before the war. One day, Jan and Knut came back from their patrol and told us they had seen a German cargo ship in the harbour in Kristiansund. The English commanding officer wanted to send the Beaufighters to attack it at once. However, the British were unsure that they could locate the specific tanker in question, and Knut offered to lead the way in his Mosquito. Ten of them went on the sortie, with Knut and Jan among them. When they approached the coastline, Knut took over the lead of the formation. Knut told the Beaufighters to prepare for attack shortly before coming straight into the harbour in question. And just as he had predicted, the cargo ship was there. They came in over the harbour completely undetected and left plenty of damage. This was down to Jan's perfect navigation, and Knut's as well. The Germans must have a had a gut feeling that something was up that day, so they had Fw 190s patrolling the area, who managed to shoot down two Beaufighters. Squadrons operating over the Norwegian coastline unfortunately suffered heavy losses. When ten went out, eight usually returned. Aircraft were usually shot down by either flak or fighters. It was tough, and extremely dangerous.

It wasn't just patrols that we lost men and aircraft to. From time to time, accidents happened in Scotland as well, especially around the airfield due to so many aircraft going up at the same time. For example, just before I left for Sumburgh, we had a nasty mishap at Leuchars. One of our Mosquitos just dived straight into the ground. It's still hard to understand what caused it, for in it was such a good pilot. We saw him coming in to land, but his speed was a little high so he went back around for another go. On his second try, he was about 100 m above the ground in front of the runway, when the big Mossie turned slowly to the left, then over onto its back, and dove straight into the ground. An enormous explosion erupted, then a fire that would not go out.

When the fire truck arrived, everything was just a mess of flames and black smoke. The ammunition on board exploded all around the rescuers. It was impossible to get anywhere close to the Mosquito. They managed to get the fire under control eventually, and when everything was over and done with, all that was left of the two crewmen were charred remains. It was hard to tell whether they had died in the fire or in the crash.

We had seen accidents before, but it had mostly been British or Canadians who bought it—chaps we knew only by their faces. We thought it was all very sad, and were sorry about what happened to them, but it never got to us as much as that specific crash did. We were shaken up whenever any of the guys in our flight were killed. We had spent every day together and come to know

The crash that hit home

The accident that Finn Eriksrud so vividly remembers was his flight's first loss of life. Mosquito DZ752 E crashed into the ground on 23 May 1943 just as he remembers it. It was Midshipman Tryggve Bjørn Schieldsøe, and the squadron's signals officer, Lt Trygve Øverli, who perished in what should have been a routine training flight. Originally, pilot Schieldsøe was supposed to go up with his navigator, Quartermaster Gunnar Helgedagsrud, as usual. But just before take-off, Helgedagsrud gave his place to Øverlie so that he could test the Mosquito's radio equipment. They came in for landing too quickly the first time around, and crashed on the runway on the second try. It is obviously speculation, but the pilot may have stalled the Mosquito, perhaps overcompensating for the excessive speed of his first approach. This was a close shave for Gunnar Helgedagsrud. After the loss of Schieldsøe, he teamed up with Midshipman Sigmund Breck. Breck was hit by a lorry in June, and written off duty for a long time. Helgedagsrud then joined Håkon Wenger in July, and ultimately became one of the longest surviving members of the flight.

and appreciate them. So this felt different. This *was* different.

After this accident, we lost the will to fly any more, at least for that day. An ill-ease had settled over us all, and we couldn't shake it off. Our flight-leader, Håkon Offerdal, understood what was going on. He called us all into

Håkon Offerdal

Offerdal was born on 31 October 1911, in Bergen, Norway. He learned to fly with the Royal Norwegian Navy before the Second World War. In 1940 he participated in the fight in western Norway, before leaving for Britain as early as 1 May. He played a leading role in the early days of Little Norway before having a short spell in Malta. He flew Catalinas with No. 333 Squadron from Woodhaven from February 1942 onwards. On 19 June, he participated in a rescue operation on the coast of Norway, evacuating three men, a woman, and a child, who were put in danger on account of a secret radio transmitter. He flew a Norwegian Catalina named 'Vingtor' on this daring mission. All crew members on this operation later received decorations for their bravery from King Haakon in London. He took charge of the Mosquito flight in 1943, which he led until his death later that year (see the flight's losses in 1943 further below for details). His remains were repatriated back to Norway after the war.

his office and expressed his sadness over what had happened.

Offerdal also told us that things like this were bound to happen. We had to deal with it, and couldn't afford to dwell on it. We had to get on with what we were doing.

Even after these words, we had trouble accepting what had happened. It felt impossible to continue with our job, or talk with each other like nothing had happened. It could have been any one of us in that Mosquito. The next day, however, we tried to put a bit of distance between us and the accident, and life gradually went back to normal, if you can call it that.

At least we knew with absolute certainty how those two chaps had died, having seen the whole thing with our own eyes. There was some comfort in knowing what had happened to them, for, from time to time, crews didn't return from Norway and no one knew what had gone down. We didn't know whether they had died or been captured. We could only guess, at least until we listened to some German radio broadcast and heard that aircraft were shot down over the coast that day. If we didn't hear anything, there were so many possibilities to ponder. They could have been shot down by flak or fighters. Their Mosquito might have been damaged and prevented them returning to Scotland, or forced them to land in the cold sea. They could be stuck somewhere in a dinghy with little chance of being found, even if we did go out to look for them. Every time we heard of a Mossie disappearing, we hoped for weeks on end that the crew had survived. But most of the time we never heard anything at all. They may just as easily have crashed into the Norwegian mountaintops, for the weather was far from perfect over there. Maybe they had simply crashed into the sea? We flew so low that it was easy to make a mistake. It seemed like anything was possible in this show, and this weighed on us greatly.

I will never forget the day Hans Olai Holdø and Jan Heide went missing. It was a Saturday afternoon in the autumn of 1943. They had left Leuchars at around two or three in the evening, and were expected back around six. Erling and I had plans to go see a film that afternoon, but suddenly got a strange feeling we had to wait until Jan and Hans came back in one piece. I don't know exactly why we wanted to wait, we had never done it before. By seven o'clock,

Flight-leader Håkon Offerdahl, Sqn Ldr Finn Lambrechts, and Knut Skavhaugen in front of a Norwegian No. 333 Squadron Mosquito, 1943. (*Forsvarsmuseet*)

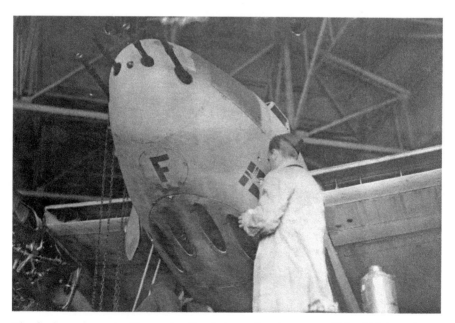

The final touches—the Norwegian flag being painted on one of No. 333 Squadron's Mosquitos. (*Forsvarsmuseet*)

we still had not heard anything of their arrival back at Leuchars either on the radio, or from the sound of Merlin engines that usually announced arrivals at Leuchars. Erling and I went to the Ops room. We saw instantly that everyone was worried about their delayed return.

As time went by that evening, we realised they had patrolled Norway for the last time. From time to time we had discussed what we would do if one of us went missing. Jan always suggested it as a good excuse for a big piss up, and insisted that this had to be done if he didn't return. We could not stay home in our beds sulking, no way. Those were his feelings about the matter. So Erling and I went to Dundee, and tried to do as Jan had told us. It was easier said than done: we gave up quickly, and went home to our beds.

Actually, we spoke very little about such matters, and when we did, it was mostly in a humorous context. We calculated the statistical chances of getting out of it with our lives intact, and ended up with a one-in-seven chance of staying alive. I think Jan sort of had a premonition he wouldn't make it. For my own part, I have to admit that I never doubted that I would be the lucky one out of seven.

Losses in 1943

Finn Eriksrud's flight suffered heavy casualties in 1943. These have been accredited to several factors since the war. Alf R. Bjercke, a ground mechanic originally from No. 332 Squadron, moved up to Leuchars to join the flight in 1943. In his opinion, part of the problem was a lack and inappropriate kind of instruction. Sqn Ldr Finn Lambrechts wanted to give his A-Flight Catalina pilots a crack at the Mosquito first, and in his eagerness also declined offers to give the pilots proper Mosquito training. Håkon Offerdal, for example, came straight from the slow flying Catalinas over to the fast Mosquito. 'There would be many destroyed Mosquitos and unnecessary funerals,' wrote Bjercke in 2001, 'before the importance of proper training dawned on the Navy pilots'.[1] Between May and August 1943, they lost a total of six Mosquitos: Schieldsøe and Øverlie in May (DZ752); Hagerup and Finne in June (DZ754, lost to flak over Norway); Sundt-Jacobsen and Aagard in July (DZ705, lost at sea); flight-leader Håkon Offerdal and his navigator Paulsen in early August (DD690, collided with an Anson over Leuchars); and Holdøe and Heide in late August (DZ745, lost to Fw 190s over Norway).

14

Hunting the *Lützow*

Our task wasn't just to search for German convoys. We also made sorties looking for large fleets of ships off the Norwegian coast.

There was plenty of fuss in the Ops room on one occasion. We were told to be ready to fly in five minutes. It turned out that all this excitement was over a German battleship named the *Lützow*. It had been observed in the morning just off Smølen, heading south at full speed. Someone had to go up and find it again to see what it was up to, and Erling and I got the job. We realised at once that this was a very risky undertaking. This battleship was escorted by many smaller naval vessels, and at least ten 190s circling around it. However, we sombrely understood that this mission had to be accomplished. If we managed to find it again, we could report back and make sure someone could go and sink it once and for all. One of the chaps came down with us to our Mosquito and joked that as long as we flew low and slow, things would turn out fine.

We would patrol between Kristiansund and Bremanger. Erling did a fantastic job with the navigation, and we made landfall just outside Kristiansund. We headed south, and followed the coast, closing in on Bremanger. The tension in the cockpit increased gradually as we got to the point where would have to head back home. Even though we hoped we could spot the battleship and report back that we had found it, I don't think either of us could deny breathing a sigh of relief when we came to Bremanger and saw nothing. We could head back to Scotland in one piece and in good conscience, knowing we had done the best we could. We didn't even meet so much as a single German fighter, when we had feared coming up against ten of them! When we came back to Leuchars and landed, we were told that the battleship had been sighted outside Haugesund. All that sweat and stress had been for nothing.

The Lützow

The *Lützow* was originally named *Deutschland*. It was launched on 19 May 1931 and commissioned two years later, assigned to 5 Group—alongside

Battleship *Lützow*. It was Eriksrud and Johanssen's task to locate it. (*Tor Idar Larsen's collection*)

heavy cruiser *Blücher* and light cruiser *Emden*—as part of Operation Weserübung, the invasion of Norway. The *Lützow* carried around 400 soldiers on its voyage to Norway, departing on 8 April 1940. On the 9th, it followed the *Blücher* into the Oslofjord. When they reached Drøbak, the *Blücher* was hit by shells and two torpedoes from the Oscarsborg Fortress. The *Lützow* was hit three times by 15-cm shells, causing significant damage. While the *Blücher* capsized, there was enough time for the Norwegian royal family and government to escape the invading forces. The *Lützow* had to retire to Germany for repair, but returned to Norway on 12 November 1942, arriving in Narvik. She participated in Operation Regenbogen in December 1942, an attack on a British arctic convoy to aid the Soviet Union's war effort. A battle commenced between German and British forces, but the Germans failed to destroy the convoy. In March 1943, the *Lützow* moved to Altafjord, where she experienced problems with her diesel engine. Once again, she had to go to Germany for repair. She returned to Norway briefly, but more overhaul was required at the end of September 1943. According to the squadron ORB, Eriksrud made a shipping recce on the 27th in the Kristiansund area, flying Mosquito HP858 K. This is most likely the sortie he refers to further below, and was in fact the only sortie Eriksrud and Johanssen made in September 1943. They made no other recce over the coast of Norway until the flight's operations started up again in November. The hunt for the *Lützow* was of the utmost importance. They were chosen for the patrol because they were in all seriousness the only remaining crew with the experience to do it. The *Lützow* arrived safely in Kiel, avoiding Eriksrud and Johanssen's hunt for it, and work on the ship lasted until January 1944. It did not return to Norway, but was sunk in 1947 as part of a weapon test by the Soviet Union.

It wasn't just the Germans we were up against over the Norwegian coast— the weather also gave us a lot of trouble. In the summer of '43, we were for the most part okay. It was a pleasure flying patrols in this kind of weather. During the winter, though, it was a totally different story. We had our orders not to continue the patrol if we ran into bad conditions. But we were all stubborn and wanted to continue, no matter how poor visibility was—not a recipe for success.

The summer and autumn of 1943 saw No. 333 Squadron's Mosquitos take a heavy beating. By the autumn, only Erling and I were left of the original seven crews who started out at Leuchars. We had just as few Mosquitos left operational: one in working order, and another which stood in a hangar at Sumburgh engineless. We had no choice but to start all over again, educate new crews, and get new Mossies. This naturally took time, though, and we

Low and fast. An air-to-air photograph of a Norwegian Mosquito. (*Forsvarsmuseet*)

weren't back in business until November 1943. I ended up as the only one of the seven original pilots to survive that summer.

In England, holidays came regularly. Every three months we would get at least a week off duty. For Erling and me it usually meant going to London. We decided twice to visit Cornwall and swim in the sea, but every time we got near London we ran into so many familiar faces that we never made it out of the city! On one such expedition I ran into Gunnar Høverstad, who was on leave at the same time as me. He had done over twenty-five sorties as a pilot in a Halifax bomber. He had been transferred to a Pathfinder squadron and enjoyed his time oh so much. His was indeed a great responsibility. His aircraft would be the first over the target and drop markers for the rest of the formation to go on. It wasn't long after my holiday that I got the news that his entire crew was missing, including Gunnar. I heard later on that the aircraft had been damaged, and that they had parachuted to safety. My sources told me that Gunnar had kept the aircraft level while the others jumped. He had no time to get out himself, though, and went down with the aircraft as the only man left inside.

Gunnar Høverstad

Gunnar Høverstad was born on 13 February 1922 in Asker, Norway. His father was school historian Torstein Høverstad, from Valdres in Oppland. He was Finn Eriksrud's best friend, and they attempted escape from Norway together in the autumn of 1940.

After a spell in Little Norway and the obligatory Operational Training Unit in Britain, he was ordered to RAF Rufforth just west of York, equipped with Handley Page Halifaxes, and the station's 1663 Heavy Conversion Unit (HCU). He arrived there two weeks before Fridtjov S. Giørtz. There were several other Norwegians with 1663 HCU as well. Gunnar was lucky, and got a fellow Norwegian on his crew: Sgt Arne Storm was a former member of No. 332 Squadron's ground crew at North Weald, who worked his way into the sky, like so many of the ground crews dreamed of doing. Giørtz speaks of their disappointment at not being sent to a Lancaster squadron and having to settle for Halifaxes. However, when they got up close to the bomber, they realised the differences were not as prominent as they first thought. A Lancaster could carry a bigger bomb load, but the Halifax was up to par in terms of both height and speed.

From 1663 HCU, Gunnar Høverstad was sent to No. 76 Squadron at Holme-on-Spolding-Moor in Yorkshire. He joined A-Flight, which also had a Norwegian flight commander, John Magne Stene. No. 76 Squadron would become the most 'Norwegian' bomber squadron of the Second World War, both in the air and on the ground. By the time Giørtz arrived, Høverstad had already finished his second dickey sortie together with fellow Norwegian

Leif Hulthin, and was ready for his first flight to Hamburg. On this occasion, Hulthin made a mistake during take-off which resulted in a burnt out wreckage and bombs explosions at the base. The crew survived.

The Norwegians at No. 76 Squadron obviously spent much time together off duty. Gunnar Høverstad and Fridtjof Giørtz played a lot of chess. In the late summer of 1943, Høverstad was transferred to No. 35 Squadron at Graveley, as part of 8 Group's Pathfinder Force—a great honour for Gunnar Høverstad. The Norwegians at No. 76 were sad to see him go.

As Finn Eriksrud wrote in 1945, he last saw his friend in London on one of his breaks from operational flying. There they met a woman named Inger T. for lunch, most likely an acquaintance of Eriksrud's family.

It is difficult to say who informed Eriksrud of his friend's death, or when. Høverstad completed over thirty missions before he went down with his Halifax on 2 December 1943 (although some sources date the crash back to the 3rd). Høverstad was still a member of No. 35 Squadron at Graveley when it happened. Høverstad had taken off at around five in the afternoon for his last sortie, in Halifax HK167 TL-C, bound for Berlin. After being hit by flak, Høverstad told his crew to abandon the stricken bomber. Everyone bailed out safely except for him. Eriksrud may have been informed of the loss by the only other Norwegian on board, Arne Storm. In 1947, Gunnar Høverstad

RAF Halifax bombers. (*Tor Idar Larsen's collection*)

A Handley Page Halifax of
the kind that Eriksrud's friend
Gunnar Høverstad operated.
(*Peter Millington's collection*)

was posthumously awarded the Norwegian War Cross with Sword for his
heroic acts that night. The rest of the aircrew consisted of the aforementioned
Norwegian Arne Storm, Flt Sgt McDougal, Sgt Brazier, Sgt Briggs, Sgt Williams, and Sgt Cooke. Eriksrud keenly felt the loss of his best friend over the
coming years.

London was obviously full of military personnel, both male and female.
You could see uniforms just about anywhere you looked. Plenty used to go
to there when they were on leave, so all hotels and B&Bs were fully booked
most of the time. It was always tricky to get a room anywhere. One evening
in London, I got talking to an American sergeant. He had been involved in a
sortie to Hamburg that very day, and seen his best friend killed by shrapnel.
He was extremely bitter and kept screaming obscene words at the Germans.
Many had been through the same as this young American, and thousands put
their lives at stake every day. It wasn't surprising that life in London was so
hectic. Many were of the opinion that you should have a good time while you
could. You could be dead the next day anyway.

The air raids on London had finished by this time. The sirens were seldom
at play. On the rare occasion that a lone German aircraft did appear over the
city, it was always low and going at full speed, before it released its bombs and
made a quick getaway. They rarely made it as far as London, though. Firstly,
the city was surrounded by extremely heavy anti-aircraft batteries; secondly,
there were always plenty of barrage balloons around to prevent these low level
raids. You never really knew when the Germans might pop over, so there were
still plenty of people spending the night in the underground. If you caught
the last tube at around midnight you could see many of them, mostly elderly,
about to make up their beds for the night.

On my first visits down to the capital, there had been a lot of people sleeping in
the tube stations. Back then the Germans were still busy over Britain. I was very

rattled the first time I experienced one of these attacks. I was at the pictures with a young girl when the film suddenly stopped and we were informed there was a raid on. Then the film started rolling again. Only a few people in the first rows decided to leave. I was stayed in my seat, but was very nervous. I wanted to ask if it might perhaps be better to leave, as the explosions kept getting closer to our location. Finally I gathered up enough courage to ask my date if we should leave, but she told me that we at least could wait until the film was over, for it was almost finished. So, I stayed put. I can't for the life of me remember anything about what was going on on screen, though. I was too busy listening to the explosions outside! The audience around me seemed perfectly calm. They laughed and had a jolly good time as sirens went off above us. I have often wondered whether this behaviour stemmed from the typically English stiff upper lip in the face of life and war, or if it was in fact a form of fatalism.

London could certainly be a fun place for a week or so, but by then I was usually sick and tired of all the people and events we got tangled up with while we were there. It was actually a relief to be at Leuchars again and to get back into to my routine. On the other hand, this could get a little tedious too, what with all the waiting around that we did. I was under the impression that most of a soldier's life consisted of waiting for something. We had to stay close to our Mossies for days on end, ready to go at 30 minutes' notice.

Finn Eriksrud after the war. (*Finn Eriksrud's collection*)

There was always something more to learn. Always new orders and new methods to get accustomed to. We were especially interested in shooting, and at every opportunity filled up our Mossies with blanks and went out flying. Crucially, it kept us on our toes. More often than not, a Mosquito came back having shot down a German over Norway. This was initially a momentous event, and we celebrated like mad. Knut Skavhaugen and Jan Heide were the first to be successful. They ran into a flying boat over Haugesund harbour and shot it down. When they came back we rejoiced like men possessed. We were all in such high spirits that night, especially Jan. He kept demonstrating to us how it all had played out. He got himself up on a chair, held his arms out, and tried to portray the German flying boat. To show us how the German went down, he dived head first onto the floor. He got up grinning, looked at his watch, and told us that the Germans had been dead for 6 hours 30 minutes and 15 seconds. He kept repeating this little show the entire evening, and calculated the time correctly each time. It showed the experience had left its mark on him.

Knut Skavhaugen and his first victory

Eriksrud remembers the flight's first victory well. It came as early as 13 June 1943, when Lt Knut Skavhaugen and PO Jan Heide shot down a Dornier Do 24T-1 flying boat just outside the town of Haugesund in Mosquito DZ700 H. The Dornier had sixteen people on board, and it crashed in the harbour area. The Dornier came from Führer-Kurierstaffel Todt. One person survived the crash. This was Skavhaugen and Heide's first operational patrol over Norway.

Knut Skavhaugen was born in 1915 in Elverum, Hedmark, in the southeast of Norway. He escaped Norway in a fishing boat named *Njål* in the early months of 1941 and arrived in Britain shortly thereafter. Over half of the men aboard *Njål* had already attempted escape the day before in a different boat. They ran into engine trouble and simply drifted back towards the shoreline, before running aground west of Vigra.

Skavhaugen stayed with the flight into the late summer of 1943. He also took charge of when Håkon Offerdal died in a mid-air collision with the Avro Anson. His last sortie with Jan Heide as navigator came on 17 August 1943. They had to immediately return to Sumburgh due to engine trouble.

Skavhaugen lost his former navigator on the 28th of August, the first loss of his command. On 6 September 1943, Skavhaugen was ordered by Finn Lambrechts, No. 333 Squadron's commanding officer, to give the flight to Haakon Jørgensen. The new flight commander had never flown a Mosquito before. Both the Norwegian and British forces were by then worried about the flight's heavy losses, for four out of six Mosquitos had already been lost. The flight carried out only one patrol between the 28th of August and 15th of November 1943, on 27 September and flown by Finn Eriksrud and Erling

Johanssen. Skavhaugen was so upset by the casualties that he requested a transfer to photo-reconnaissance. He ended up at a desk job in London within a month. Four months later, he had enough, and applied to return to active duty in the RAF.

On 10 June 1944, Skavhaugen joined No. 107 Squadron of the Second Tactical Air Force, which supported the allied armies on the continent after D-Day. The British quickly spotted his potential as a pilot and a leader, and he became flight commander. He flew fifty-six operational sorties with No. 107 Squadron, then was sent on mandatory leave in late November 1944. Meanwhile, the Norwegians laid plans to return him back to No. 333 Squadron, which Skavhaugen accepted. Lambrecht had also left No. 333 Squadron by then, which might also have motivated Skavhaugen to come back. After five sorties, he became flight commander of No. 333 B-Flight and its Mossies once more.

On 25 March 1945, Knut Skavhaugen made his final sortie. He and his navigator, Fg Off. Arnold Hannam Bobbet served as outriders for a large Mosquito offensive escorted by RAF Mustangs from the Banff Strike Wing. A large German tanker had been observed going south along the Norwegian coast, and the Banff Strike Wing split into two groups in search of it. Skavhaugen led one group around Sognefjorden and Askvoll in Mosquito HR141 G.

They found nothing of interest and turned back towards Banff. The group was then attacked by twenty-four Focke Wulf Fw 190s from Herdla airfield. Knut and his navigator were pursued by three of them, coming in from behind and with superior speed. The Mosquito spun into the sea in flames. About sixty aircraft were involved in the dogfight that followed over Alden and Bulandet. The Germans lost five Fw 190s, and the Banff Strike Wing a Mustang and two Mosquitos, including HR141 G.

Skavhaugen was always considered 'one of the boys'. He was a well-liked officer, someone whom everyone looked up to, which was not the case for all officers in No. 333 Squadron. Finn Andvig, a Mosquito pilot in the northern group of the Banff Strike Wing that day, latterly expressed bitterness at how things turned out in an interview:

The weather was pretty bad when I arrived. I fly past this small island called Alden. It was a well-used landmark, a square-looking big rock. On its northern side I saw fire in the sea. Someone had died there. When we came back home, Skavhaugen was not there. I never heard what happened. Three aircraft went down, together with him and an Englishman. It's strange that I haven't really heard anything. He was popular, our boss at the time. A damn, damn good chap. A bloody good guy, you know, whereas Lambrechts was an arrogant prick.[1]

Ground crew sorting out the ammunition for another sortie to Norway. (*Forsvarsmuseet*)

Preparing for another patrol over Norway. (*Forsvarsmuseet*)

There are three photographs which show the Junkers Ju 88 crashing into the sea after being attacked by Finn Eriksrud and Erling Johanssen. Take special notice of the wingtip streamer. (*Finn Eriksrud's collection*)

A second photograph of Finn Eriksrud and Erling Johanssen's catch. The Junkers Ju 88 is clearly on fire; its elevator pulled its weight in giving it lift, but to no avail. (*Finn Eriksrud's collection*)

The third and last in the series of known photographs of the incident. In this one you can clearly see the Mosquito's bank and wing. (*Finn Eriksrud's collection*)

The attack on the Junkers 88

Eriksrud neglects to mention one of the most photographed 'kills' by any Norwegian pilot during the Second World War. November 22nd was certainly a day to remember. With the flight filled with fresh crews, operations over the Norwegian coast had now started again. Finn Eriksrud took his regular navigator Erling Victor Johanssen and Mosquito HP860 marked 'R' on a recce in the Stavanger–Lista area. At around 10 a.m., they sighted a Junkers Ju 88 (D7+BH) at 2,000 feet and at a 130-degree angle. The weather was cloudy, and the Germans kept flying in and out of the clouds. Finn chased the Junkers down and opened fire from dead astern. Pieces flew off the fuselage, and one of the engines caught fire. When Eriksrud flew past the aircraft, Johanssen took up his camera and snapped photos of the doomed German. The Junkers then glided down towards the sea and disappeared into the dark waters. Finn Eriksrud had scored his second German kill, and a formidable one at that.

15

The Last Sortie

Winter had started to creep up on us at Leuchars. Lots of rain, bad weather, and little flying. One afternoon, when it finally had cleared up enough for flying, Erling and I went on a patrol from Stavanger to Bergen. That morning, fellow pilot Andreas Wyller had told me that he dreamt that I fell into the sea. We joked and laughed it off as usual, and I didn't think more of it until later on.

Erling and I headed out of Scotland much as we had done so many times before. Ten kilometres away from the Norwegian coast, we ran into a terrible winter storm. The wind became so violent, and we flew though some horrid hail. We could not for anything see much beyond 100 m ahead. According to our schedule, we should have been at the Norwegian coastline before long. We decided to keep going for a few more minutes, but if we were still not clear of the storm we would have to turn back home. It was hopeless to conduct a patrol in that weather. Seconds before we agreed to turn back, it cleared up, and we realised we were deep into the Boknafjord. We turned north, and flew by Karmøysundet past Haugesund, where the Germans did their usual thing, though with no real success. The weather worsened once again when we reached our turning point, and we decided to fly south. We figured we could have missed something going north due to the weather. We also thought we could relax when it came to Germans in the air. They wouldn't send any fighter after us in this terrible weather, we were sure of it. We had twice flown past Bommelømen, and still no improvement weather-wise. We decided to head back home, and were on the right course for about 1½ minute when Erling noticed an unknown aircraft cutting across our course. It turned out to be a Heinkel He 111. We could not have wished for an easier target than this. The Mossie was completely superior to this slow bomber.

We attacked them from their port side. I fired both cannons and machine guns. If I hit the Heinkel, I was sure it would go down. After the first strike, pieces were flying off its rudder. I decided to go around and try again. I pressed the firing button once again, and this time a big red flame came out of one of the Heinkel's engines. The slow bomber was doomed. Our delight was premature, however. It turned out that this Heinkel also had its own ammunition on board. As we passed underneath it after our attack, we got caught all of the smoke and fire over of us. We couldn't see a thing. At the last second I pushed the stick forward and the Mossie nipped between the doomed Heinkel and the rough sea. The attack was a success, and we had done everything right. We kept firing while heading straight at him, and then moving away at the last possible moment. All we had to do was get out in one piece ourselves. All that excitement and tension distracted us our own vulnerability.

We had just passed the Heinkel when we discovered that our starboard engine had been hit. So, the German gunner had managed to get in a few good shots after all. Just a second later or so, our starboard engine seized up completely, and a river of fuel flowed over the wing. I stopped the engine, and feathered the propellers. Erling kept a close eye on the Heinkel, which was still flying. I had more than enough to keep me preoccupied, what with keeping the Mosquito in the air. Erling kept a cool head and calmly told me what was happening over the radio.

'It's about to hit the sea,' he told me, 'gliding very slowly now. A dark flame. There, it hit the sea. A big splash.'

Our port engine then played up as well, no longer running as it was supposed to. We decided halfway to try and head for Leuchars anyway, on one engine. It was very hard to know what to do. The oil pressure was low, and the engine temperature continued to climb. This was not looking good.

I never made a decision about whether to return home—the Mosquito made it for me. The temperature was now above critical, so Leuchars was out of the question. We couldn't do anything other than head back to the coastline and try to make a forced landing somewhere. To end up in a small dinghy in the North Sea did not appeal much to either of us. Bømlo, north of Haugesund, appeared ahead of us. I very much doubted we could even reach the coast, for the one running port engine was rapidly deteriorating, as we crawled back towards Norway. We couldn't use the radio to send any messages, either. It had been shot up by a very talented German gunner.

It was simply a question of landing the Mosquito as gently on the water, and as close to land, as possible. This was our only chance, anyway: taking to our parachutes was impossible due to our height. Our Mossie was just metres above the sea by then.

Erling and I strapped in as best as we could and opened the hatch above our heads, to give ourselves the best chance of getting out of the Mosquito as soon as we were down. Judging by the instruments, it was a miracle one of the port engines was running at all. It had to be a straight-forward landing. No upwind landing or anything like that. We seemed to be in luck, though, for the wind was calm, and the sea looked decently close to land. If I had had to deal with a rough sea as well, I am not sure how this would have ended.

Our Mossie hit the water just like a flying boat. The wheels were still neatly tucked inside. We skidded across the sea at tremendous speed. After about 100 m, the two engines gave up entirely and went under water. We came to a brutal stop. In the space of 100 m, our speed was reduced from about 115 to 0 mph. Thankfully, the straps held. Neither Erling nor I was injured in the slightest. We felt a bit dizzy, but that was all.

The Mossie had come in contact with the water skidding to the right, so I ended up on top of Erling, still in my seat. I got out of the open hatch, and blew air into my Mae West. The dinghy, usually placed inside the fuselage, was floating in the water. The only thing I had to do was inflate it. Erling also got out of the still half-floating Mosquito. He had had difficulty releasing himself from the straps, and the cockpit had been filled up with sea water. His face was rather blue when he popped up. We got into the dinghy and ditched our parachutes in the sea. Several of our maps were floating around us. We gathered as much as we could find, and destroyed them. We were still doing this when a rowing boat approached us. It had two Norwegian boys in it. We got on board, and while they rowed away we saw the Mosquito sink, nose first, into the cold sea. The whole tail had broken off on impact and was floating alone a bit further away from us. It was strange to see our wonderful machine disappear into the depths. We had used this Mossie on most of our patrols, and the last of the original Mosquitos' flight were now all gone. We were also the last of the flight's original personnel. All the others had been killed. We were still alive, though, even though we were out of the game. We knew others would take our place.

A rare photograph of a Norwegian Mosquito in flight—these are few and far between. (*Forsvarsmuseet*)

Finn Eriksrud and Erling Johanssen's last patrol

Eriksrud flew Mosquito Mk VI HP861 N with navigator Johanssen on his last patrol to Norway on 16 December 1943. They took off from Wick for a shipping recce, and were airborne at 1.44 p.m. After Scotland, nothing more was heard from Eriksrud and Johanssen, and they were simply noted down as failed to return. Sometime after the war, Eriksrud was given a piece of the propeller of his Mosquito by divers attempting to locate the wreck. It is now in his son's collection of memorabilia from his father's time with No. 333 Squadron. The propeller piece was the biggest object they found. Eriksrud ended the war with three confirmed victories.

Once again, the Norwegians had mistaken the identity of their target. Researchers have established that they had in fact engaged a Focke Wulf Fw 85 Weihe marked KR+CW, and not a Heinkel He 111. The Fw 85 did not return to base, thus concluding Finn Eriksrud's total score of three confirmed victories.

Erling Johanssen's escape from the doomed Mosquito was much more dramatic than what Finn Eriksrud wrote in 1945. According to Johanssen, he nearly lost the battle to release himself from the straps. Eriksrud actually had to pull his navigator out of the Mosquito by his hair. Johanssen survived quite literally by a hair's breadth, and was always convinced that Eriksrud saved his life on that fateful day. He is more than likely right.

After rowing about 100 m, we were brought up to a small white house. The people there were shocked when they realised we were Norwegians. We asked whether there were any quislings around. The people said there were none, but the Germans did have an observation post located on a small island just a little further south.

Our time at sea had left us terribly frozen. We took off our wet clothes and borrowed some dry ones from the people from the white house.

As we were standing there in our underwear, about ten Germans arrived and told us we were prisoners of war. We acknowledged that this was indeed the case and came to terms with the situation at hand. They searched us, and looked through all our wet clothes. They were a tad late though, we had already burnt everything of interest in the oven. It was standard policy to destroy anything of interest to the Germans—everything that had to do with where we came from, and what type of mission we were on.

The Norwegians then told us they had had no option but to denounce us to the Germans and local police. At first we couldn't understand why they would do such a thing, but after a while we realised that, since they had an outpost close by, the Germans had probably witnessed the whole thing. The locals had simply informed them of what was going on to keep out of trouble. It wouldn't have made much difference, either way. These people were fishermen, and very kind. We got to keep the clothes we borrowed until ours were dry again. They offered us coffee and cakes as well—it being December, the locals were preparing for Christmas by baking all sorts of cakes and cookies. Lucky for us.

Afterwards, we had to go with the Germans. We boarded a small fishing boat, and were brought to this observation post we had heard so much about. They offered us some food, and then we were put into a room with one bed. Erling and I would share this room for the night. I don't think I would have been able to sleep even if it had been comfortable. My mind kept wandering to everyone at Leuchars and how they must have been asking themselves what on earth had happened to us.

I had invited a young girl from Dundee to the Christmas dance at the station that evening. We had already agreed that I would pick her up that afternoon. I hoped Andreas Wyller remembered my date, and would call to tell her that it was sadly cancelled. I did have a valid reason not to attend. She would probably have to wait a while before I returned.

It was maddening to be captured like this, but both of us took comfort in the fact that everything might have turned out so much worse. We could have gone straight into the sea, stuck in our Mossie—the German Heinkel had done just that, no one had got out of it. Andreas's dream before our patrol had certainly been fulfilled.

Andreas Hofgaard Wyller

Andreas Wyller was born on 23 October 1919 in Oslo. He was one of Norway's best alpine skiers in the 1930s, and was crowned national champion twice. He was part of the same batch of pupils as Fridtjof Giørtz and Finn Eriksrud, arriving in July 1943 and commencing training on the Mosquito shortly thereafter. He flew his first recce on 15 November 1943. Wyller stayed with the flight until his death on 23 February 1944. Giørtz was one of Wyller's closest friends and had been ordered to Leuchars to join the civilian Stockholm route to Bromma (Sweden) and back, flying Lockheed Lodestars. He solemnly recounts how he learned of his friend's death:

> As a civilian I would not stay at Leuchars, but in St. Andrews. Together with Per Bugge, who had done a whole tour flying Bristol Beaufighters, we rented a room at the Star Hotel and got settled in there on the 23rd. After getting organised, I went up to Leuchars to say hello to Andreas Wyller. In my letters to him I had not mentioned that I would be stationed at Leuchars from now on—I wanted to surprise him. In the Ops room I was told he was out on a recce, but that they expected him back any minute.
>
> It turned out to be a long wait. At length, Ops had to accept that Andreas

was lost. Their fuel load would by then be long gone.

I was rather downcast when I took the bus back to St. Andrews that day. I wondered if Andreas had managed to jump out and got away with his life intact, or if all his dreams for the future were done for. We had just decided our friendship would last after the war, as well. I was under strict orders to find a wife who could play bridge. Andreas had already chosen one somewhere.

The next day I listened to the news, and heard on the radio that the Germans bragged about shooting down a Mosquito over the coast of Norway. They didn't say a word about what happened to Andreas. Later on, the sad news reached me—he had been killed.[1]

The Mosquito flown by Wyller and his navigator Bård Carl Benjaminsen was most likely shot down by a Junkers Ju 88 in a dogfight over Eigerøya, not far from Egersund. The Ju 88 was also lost in the encounter. Wyller had two victories at the time of his death. The Mosquito may also have been fighting Fw 190s, but it is more commonly accepted that they were shot down by the Ju 88.

In the 1930s, Wyller created 'The Wyller Slope', an alpine skiing slope in Sørkedalen, Oslo. It was officially opened in 1956 and is still there today. A memorial to Andreas Wyller was erected close by in 1994.

Andreas Hofgaard Wyller in training in Canada. (*Fridjof Giørtz's collection*)

16

Prisoner of War

At some point in the morning I finally fell asleep. When I woke up, I had trouble knowing where I was. I didn't recognise any of the surroundings—neither the little hard bed I was on nor all the potato bags stacked up against a wall. Then I saw Erling beside me, still sleeping. It all came back to me.

A German guard came in and told us to follow him. He explained to me that they had received orders not to keep Erling and me in the same room, and that we weren't allowed to talk to each other. We stayed in the German observation post under guard the entire day, puzzling over where we would be taken next. We pretended not to speak German. With the use of my hands I tried asking the guard where we would be taken.

'Well,' he said, 'tomorrow a boat will come and pick you up and take you to Bergen.' That was all that he knew, apparently. The next night I got a bed to myself, so I slept better.

We got our uniforms back the following day. They were all dry now. We got out of our civilian clothes, and the Germans promised to give them back to the right owners. Around noon a small naval vessel came and brought us to Bergen, like the guard had told us. Erling was placed in a small room at the back of the ship, while I got a room at the front. I shared it with three or four German sailors. They were quite nice, and I ate the best Lapskaus I had ever tasted with them. They also gave me a few cigarettes. One of them told me in all seriousness he had volunteered to join the German invasion of England, which was due within a couple of months. He didn't doubt for one second that he would soon be walking around in London smoking Chesterfields.

I noticed my trousers would be a problem, for buttons were missing in crucial places. I asked them if they had a few to spare, which they did.

When we finally arrived in Bergen it was already dark. We were picked up at the harbour by a German officer and four soldiers, and taken straight to the prison. This was the first place they asked us anything at all. They seemed pleased when we only gave them our names, rank, and service number. They never gave much thought to getting more information out of us.

It was still dark the next morning when were woken up. We were quickly rushed to the railway station in a car, where a Christmas tree was all lit up, and painfully reminded us that there was a holiday going on around us. I don't really think anyone took much notice of our uniforms. I guessed they figured we were German soldiers. We observed this in their attitude to us: apathy. They didn't even bother looking at us, which actually pleased us both. The general mood in Bergen was far from sympathetic towards the occupying forces. Erling and I were then led into an empty cart, where we spent the rest of the time with four new German soldiers. They all looked rather angry and rough around the edges. They all had their machine guns and kept playing with them. I don't know if it was an old habit they had or if it was to show us what would happen if we tried to make a run for it. Wherever we went, they followed us with their machine guns at the ready. Any small hope I had of escaping sank to an all-time low.

It was to be a day of sunshine and superb weather. We got a lovely trip across the mountains from Bergen to Oslo, and both spent most of the time staring out the window. Just looking at the awesome nature outside made me feel better at heart. When we passed Geilo, where I had spent so many Easter holidays, my heart sank a little again. I couldn't help but think about the unfortunate mess I had got myself into.

We arrived at Drammen railway station the same afternoon. I don't know the cause of it, but we were told the train did not go any further. I got the impression that the railway line was either faulty or had been sabotaged somewhere between Drammen and Oslo. While we waited to be taken to Oslo by car, we had to spend some time in a German office waiting for a car to pick us up. There were plenty of Germans around, and we caused quite a stir. At first we were mistaken for German deserters, and a lively discussion started to evolve around us. One of our guards managed to get in a word, telling them we were Norwegian POWs. The situation calmed down considerably after that, but we didn't enjoy our stay one bit. We also discovered two Gestapo officers at the other end of the room, so we were far from pleased with all this mess. We could only hope those two wouldn't get involved in anything. Luckily, the car came after half an hour's wait, and took us to Fornebu airfield outside Oslo. There we were separated into two cells. Mine had an iron bed, two blankets, a table, and a small chair. I was exhausted by then, and fell asleep at once.

Fornebu Airfield

Fornebu was Oslo's main airfield from 1939 until 1998, when operations moved to Gardermoen, north of Oslo. The first aircraft to land at Fornebu was a Junkers Ju 52 operated by Lufthansa. It had been on a scheduled route to Kjeller outside Lillestrøm, when the captain took a detour to check out the new airfield. As part of the invasion of Norway in 1940, it took as little as the Luftwaffe landing their aircraft there to seize Fornebu. They had no other choice, besides, since their fuel had at this stage reached a critical level. In the hours before the airfield fell into German hands, the Norwegian Army Air Force had operated seven Gloster Gladiators and met the invading air force head-on from there. These Norwegians were led by Rolf Torbjørn Tradin (later a No. 611 Squadron pilot, and KIA in 1943). One Gladiator landed back at Fornebu after running out of ammunition, while the others either crashed or force landed elsewhere. None of the Norwegian pilots were killed. They shot down several German aircraft, but could not hinder their advance to Fornebu. On the 12th of April, the British bombed the airfield. At the north end of the runway, the Luftwaffe built several hangars and a prison camp. Prisoners were used to keep the runways free of snow during the wintertime by marching up and down the runway and stomping the snow down with their feet. Eriksrud mentions seeing prisoners working outside in his book, and may have been imprisoned at the north end of the airfield.

I spent the next day familiarising myself with the surroundings. Erling turned out to be my neighbour, in the cell just down the hallway. He was quickly moved, so we ended up separated with one cell between us. Opposite us was a German soldier imprisoned for some kind of disciplinary matter. I was disappointed in the view though. I could only look straight down into a large hole in the ground. Russian prisoners kept digging it under the supervision of a big and ruthless looking German guard.

As a matter of fact, this was familiar territory for me. I had been to Fornebu many times before the war. However, it didn't really matter how close I was to home. I might as well have been thousands of miles away. No one knew I was here, and I couldn't go outside to talk to anybody. I debated trying to send some kind of greeting back home for a while, but decided against it. Looking back, I think I made the right choice. I was soon afterwards very pleased that I hadn't brought my family into all of this. I had also determined to keep in good physical shape while in German captivity. For all I knew, it might come in handy. So, to the entertainment of the German guard outside, I did half an hour of gymnastics each morning.

They visited Erling's cell on the very first afternoon. After a while they came back, and it was my turn. I was taken to a large villa just outside the airfield's boundaries, and presented to a lieutenant and a corporal equipped with pencil and paper. The lieutenant asked me about my name, rank, and service number. He then started to chat an awful lot about this and that. It was obvious he wanted to portray himself as a very nice gentleman. He was very upset about the recent bombing of Hamburg. I remarked that several Norwegian towns were bombed into oblivion during the invasion in 1940.

'Well, yes, but that is totally different,' he told me, 'they were military targets, and Hamburg is not.'

I didn't want to discuss the matter further with him. Firstly, it seemed useless, and secondly, I had a feeling he *wanted* me to discuss these things with him. He spoke excellent English, but from time to time changed to German to see if I reacted and understood what he said. After this he started to ask me questions of obvious military interest. I kept telling him that he knew as much as I did, that I could not answer those questions, and could not give him more than what I had already told him. He became increasingly angry, and threatened me. Especially about the Gestapo. He also told me that he knew for a fact that I had left Norway after the occupation had started, and that if I did not behave myself, he would treat me like a traitor. It was up to me, he said, to deal with the consequences. However, if I were to give him just a little bit of useful information, he would make sure the Gestapo would not touch me, and that I would be transported to a POW camp.

In the middle of questioning, a German major entered the room. He did not understand English, so he and the lieutenant spoke in German. I understood by their conversation that I would be taken to some sort transit camp the Luftwaffe had in Frankfurt. I had heard about this camp in England, and I knew all pilots had to go through this place sooner or later after capture. This new information calmed me greatly, and I concluded there would be no Gestapo.

When both of the Germans realised I would not speak, the lieutenant started to tell me which squadron I belonged to. He got some of it right, but far from everything. There were several details about which he was remarkably on point. I would be even more surprised when I was in Frankfurt and shown a folder full of information and photographs of a Mosquito and its performance under various conditions. The documents were signed by an English colonel. The date was pretty recent too, so it seemed to me that this information had come straight from an airfield in England. It could have been a hoax, but I don't believe this was the case.

After my interrogation at the villa outside Fornebu, I was returned to my cell by the lieutenant. He told me he was engaged to a Norwegian girl. He was upset that she had no friends, and could not understand why this was. The whole thing really baffled him, it seemed. I didn't bother enlightening him. If he stayed in the country for long enough, he would surely come to understand why.

The next few days were quiet and calm, except for a small episode with a German guard who did not like me standing on my chair looking at the work going on outside. I also spent Christmas Eve at Fornebu. A year ago, in 1942, I had bet Andreas Wyller a bottle of whisky that I would be back home for Christmas by now. Well, I had won the bet. I doubt he would agree, though. It wasn't as I had pictured it, but I did think I had earned the bottle!

Christmas Eve allowed for an extra treat—a small bag of sweets. Erling and I wished each other a Merry Christmas through the guard, as we were not allowed to see or talk to each other.

At first, time passed by so slowly. There was nothing to do but lie on my back and stare at the ceiling. I heard the guard's footsteps all day and all night, his iron heels against the stone floor outside. He never stopped. The sound would pass my cell, then come back. It never ever stopped. It was enough to make a man go bonkers. From time to time the marching would pause, and I knew he was looking at me through a small hole in the door. It was a tiny wall, so while he could see me, I could not see him.

One day, I overheard a conversation between two of the guards which made me nervous. They usually discussed my destiny very openly and loudly, and I had got used to it. I understood it was only their opinion of me, and nothing to worry much about. Most of them thought that I should be shot on sight for being a Norwegian, since Norway and Germany were not at war per se. That was their opinion. Some of them were on my side, and said that they couldn't shoot me as I was in uniform when I was caught, and therefore a regular soldier.

This time around though, I remember the guard telling his superior that there had been plans to send Erling to a prison camp in Germany since he had left Norway before the invasion. I, on the other hand, would be shot, as I had escaped Norway after their arrival. I started to seriously consider how serious this was, but reminded myself of this transit camp in Frankfurt that the German major had told me about. I already knew there were at least ten Norwegians in captivity in Germany. They had been shot down over the continent somewhere, but to me this made no difference.

New Year's Eve brought a great party to our tiny corner of the airfield. Plenty of noise all night, screaming and loud talking. I can't say for sure, but I have a feeling it was Norwegian girls who were entertaining that night. I got my own little pleasure out of it, though. When I was out in the hallway cleaning my socks, I snuck a peek at a newspaper that reported that the *Scharnhorst* had been sunk. I was not allowed to read anything, but I managed to smuggle the newspaper into the cell with me. The guards were looser than usual that evening, and I had a wonderful time.

The first day of the New Year brought beautiful weather. I could hear people outside ice-skating. Every day at around 4 o'clock in the afternoon, I could also hear a boat coming by and would have bet good money that it was the good old *Duen II*. I had ridden that boat a hundred times each summer.

17

Germany

In the early morning on the 3rd of January, I was woken up by an *Oberfeldwebel* [a sergeant]. He told me to get ready. It didn't take me long. I had nothing more than what I was on me. For the umpteenth time he told me that I would be shot if I gave even the slightest hint of trying to escape. I was then placed on a bus, this time with three Germans guarding me. We drove down to the America Line harbour. There was a big German ship, with lots of German soldiers on board waiting to go home. We sailed for three days, and I couldn't avoid ending up in discussions with the Germans. One of them appeared to come from a posh family. He had plenty of education, but was still a die-hard Nazi. On one occasion, we started to talk about Norwegian girls. I asked him what his opinion was.

'Well,' he hesitated before he continued, 'they are very sweet and charming, but it's been impossible for me to meet the kind I would like to be seen with.'

This was music to my ears.

Many of the Germans on board had not been home for several years. They kept talking about all the things they would do as soon as they came back home. My guards had to deliver me to the right people in Frankfurt before they could go to their families. They told me it was a top notch camp, with plenty of food and good entertainment.

It was sad leaving Norway, even though I had only been a prisoner there. I was really depressed when we sailed through the Oslofjord. Outside Moss we joined a large convoy. Plenty of mines about in these waters, so things went slowly. We anchored up in Aarhus, Denmark. A large crowd of Danes greeted us at the harbour. They showed up with apples and baked goods, which they exchanged for cigarettes. My guard bought a bag of apples, and sat there scoffing it in front of my face.

The rest of the journey was by train. It was terrible because it was so busy. Only German officers and soldiers. Not a good journey at all. It was also very cold, so I suffered greatly. We would change trains in Hamburg. I had to agree with the German lieutenant about the bombing and its effectiveness. It had been very effective indeed. From my window on the train, all I could see was rubble. Some foundations were left, and a wall here and there, but inside there was nothing but empty space. The railway station itself was in terrible condition. The entire roof had fallen down. Most of the people looked at me with murderous expressions on their faces. They most likely mistook me for one of those *Terrorflieger*. I truly hoped my stay at the railway station would be as short as was humanly possible. I also hoped the Americans would lay off bombing the city while I was in it. I had barely finished this thought before the alarm went off. People ran off to the nearest shelter. I had no choice but to follow my guards to an underground tunnel. Lots of people were gathered there, and none of them looked very friendly. I retreated back to a corner of the tunnel, and at the same time asked one of my guards if he wanted me to carry his backpack. He agreed, and let me take it. It served as the perfect camouflage. At the same time I spoke German to my guards so people around me wouldn't start wondering who I was. I was happy that I had, by that time, not heard the stories I would later be told—how civilians attacked aircrews coming down in their parachutes, and that some of these unlucky chaps were simply torn apart by the population in pure rage. This was especially liable to happen if they were caught shortly after a bombing raid. That people behaved like this after they had lost their homes, their family members, and so forth is perhaps understandable. It happened in London too, when the German bombing was at its worst.

An Englishman later told me that he came down in the middle of Berlin while the attack was still going on. Luckily, he was caught by Luftwaffe personnel and well treated after that. To get him through the city in one piece, they gave him a German uniform. This was the only way to keep him stay safe from the population. Another pilot asked his guards if they would protect him should the mob attack him.

'I cannot open fire on my fellow countrymen, but you can have my machine gun and defend yourself the way you see fit,' the guard had answered.

Those aircraft over Hamburg were going somewhere else, so all went well. We couldn't travel further that day, so spent the night in Hamburg in a loft somewhere. That same evening, some American pilots arrived. They had just been caught, and looked horrible. One's leg seemed to be in a very bad state, but he received no help.

In my humble opinion, the Germans treated the English and the Americans differently. The Americans usually had an 'eye for an eye', 'tooth for a tooth' kind of approach to things, and they never held back. The Germans hated them more than the English for this reason. The English were calmer, and never appeared as confrontational as the Americans. I got the impression most of the Germans were actually sorry to be at war with Britain, and looked upon the Brits with more favour.

We arrived in Frankfurt and the famous transit camp the next evening. Lots of barracks situated in a large space surrounded by barbed wire. Each barracks contained many small cells, and each cell had a bed with two blankets. That's all there was. I quickly learned that I had Americans in each of my neighbouring cells. I had no window to speak of, so had no idea what was going on outside. So far I had been well treated food-wise, but that was about to end. I got two slices of bread in the morning, a plate of vegetable soup in the afternoon, and another two slices of bread in the evening with a cup of coffee.

The first two days were quiet, and there were no incidents. On the third day, a German came into the neighbouring cell. At first it was hard to understand what they were talking about. The German did not get the intel he wanted from the American, and gradually raised his voice. I remember the German saying something about 'being careful' to the American. He was after all Jewish, and if he did not fill out a certain form, the Gestapo would take over. The American kept refusing, and got so upset he started to cry. The German gave him one last chance. If he didn't sign now, he would call in the Gestapo immediately. They would be there within half an hour. The American did not give in.

'You have brought this upon yourself!' the German screamed, and left the cell.

I waited tensely for the Gestapo's arrival. Was this real or just another threat? The half hour came and went. Another two hours, and still nothing. I kept waiting for them the next day as well, but no Gestapo came. In the end the American left the camp in the afternoon with about fifty other Americans. I felt relieved. This whole business with the Gestapo turned out to be a lie. It was good to know, in case I would be up for the same treatment.

Sure thing, the next day I was visited by the same German. At first he was very friendly and nice. He told me it was interesting to meet a Norwegian given that we were of the same race and therefore like family. I had to smile at this comment. What a great example of his race he was—short, fat, wearing glasses, and as bald as they come. A great Aryan indeed.

After lots of talk about Norway and how shameful it was that Norway and Germany did not stick together in this war, he put forward a document with a Red Cross symbol in the left corner. He said he would be delighted to let my family know I was okay. So, if I would be so kind to fill out the form I would be doing both him and myself a large favour. I filled out my rank, service number, and name of course, but this was not enough for him. He told me to fill out which RAF station I came from, the squadron number, and lots of other military questions. It gradually dawned on him that I would not fill in more than what I already had. He worked himself into a massive rage. His face developed a dark red colour. I thought the man would only have seconds left to live with all this rage inside, and I felt rather sorry for him. If he was doing this stuff thirty times a day, he must be exhausted every evening. It could not be good for his blood pressure, either. I decided not to touch on this subject, as I am sure I would have shortened his life by yet another month or two. He left none the wiser.

I was left alone for another week, but one afternoon was taken to another building for a repeat of the whole show. Another German was in charge this time around. In the end, he read from several documents and answered the questions himself when I refused to cooperate.

Later on I met an American who went through the exact same thing. They told him the date he had reported for duty, how long he had stayed on the different courses, the name of the airfield he was stationed at, the date he came to Britain, and how many sorties he had done. It was obvious the Germans had good intelligence from the UK. We could only hope the Allies were doing an equal job over here. Later on I also heard a story about how, in the Battle of Britain, the Brits had got crucial information out of a German pilot. When they searched him it turned out he had several letters from a young lady on him. It turned out this German was married, and that these letters were not from his wife at all. The letters turned out to be very useful. When the German refused to open up, the English interrogation officer threatened to send these love letters back to his wife. The German begged the Englishman not to send them. Well, if he answered the questions, he would get them back. So every time the German gave the Englishman information, he got one of the letters back. By the time he had retrieved them all, the English had all the information they needed. Good show!

Most of the allied pilots who came down over the continent were taken care of by the Luftwaffe, but some who had been on the run for some time could end up in the hands of the Gestapo. My impression was that the Luftwaffe did what they could to leave them out of it. Hundreds of pilots were badly mistreated by the Gestapo.

During my two weeks in Frankfurt, I was told I would be transported to a camp outside the city. I was happy to finally be out of the cell. Hours felt like days in there, and hunger had been a perpetual problem. Both the neighbouring cells from mine had a much quicker turnover of inmates, and I didn't understand how everyone but me could so expediently be on their way. I later heard that pilots the Germans thought had sensitive information were kept in these cells for three to four months. Not exactly in line with the rules on keeping POWs.

I got my watch back eventually, taken from me when I arrived in the camp. It didn't work anyway, due to all the sea water. The pen that I had kept with me was in working order, but I never saw it again.

I met Erling again as well. He had left Fornebu two days after I did. He looked terrible; much thinner, and with a full beard. Absolutely dreadful. I guess I was no better myself. I had been speculating wildly about where he had gone. I had not seen him since the day we came to Fornebu, so I was glad of the reunion.

From this camp outside the city we travelled in groups of a hundred. Erling and I were counted as English and had to wait a week. The Americans only waited for a couple days, since so many of them kept coming in each day due to their large bombing raids.

In comparison to British bombers, a relatively large proportion of air crew got out of hit American bombers. There were several reasons for this. The Americans only flew during the daytime to make it easier for them to get out in time. They also flew in formation, and if one was hit it left the formation. The pilot often lowered the undercarriage as a sign of surrender, after which they bailed out in peace and quiet as the Germans held their fire.

The British, on the other hand, flew at night. It was harder to bail out in darkness, and they could continue their sortie even after being hit under its cover, anyway. The result was more than often that the crew kept the bomber flying until there was no more time left to bail out. If I am not mistaken, the British estimated that two out of ten men were safe under these circumstances, whereas the Americans estimated around six out of ten.

In this camp we received little Red Cross packages for the first time, and I can honestly say that had it not been for them, we would have been rather skinny upon our return home. That first meal was quite an experience, after all those days of literally nothing to eat. We ate corned beef, raisins and chocolate, and crackers and butter in-between. Frankfurt was raided a few times while we were there, and we didn't feel much love for those bombers. Luckily, we got out before the entire city was turned into an even bigger pile of rubble and bricks.

18

Stalag Luft III

My journey would now continue to Stalag Luft III Bellaria, a POW camp outside the city of Sagan in Oberschlesien, about 170 km south-east of Berlin. There were three large prison camps around Sagan. Together they held about 10,000 officers belonging either to British or American forces. Bellaria was a relatively new camp. There were only fifty prisoners there when we arrived. They had been there for about two weeks, cleaning up and making it ready for when the rest of us got there. There were a total of seven barracks, plus a very shabby one used as our little theatre. Each barracks was split up into fourteen rooms. In the beginning we were eight men to a room. We slept in bunks, one atop the other. When it became twelve to a room, they added another bunk on top of the other two.

Letters home

Throughout his stay in Bellaria, Finn wrote home to his parents and relatives. The first letter was handwritten on a small piece of standard *Kriegsgefangenen-lager* cardboard. It had room for seven lines of writing—not much. He wrote a few letters in English as well. Eriksrud shares the news of Gunnar Høverstad's death in his very first letter (see Appendix: Letters Home). This was clearly a devastating loss he wanted to relay back home as quickly as possible, probably because Høverstad came from the same part of Oslo as himself.

Upon our arrival at camp we were brought into the office of a English colonel, the oldest of the allied officers, and questioned by him. We had to prove one way or another that we were those we said we were. Erling and I had no trouble doing so because one of the prisoners actually was a friend of mine from Canada, and we spent a lot of time together there. The background check was essential, since the Germans would on occasion put their own people in the camp disguised as English officers, in order to find out what we were up to. They took special interest in our tunnel-digging projects, and where they were located. They also wanted to know if and where we had radios. But these spies were always unmasked, and the Germans requested to remove them at once, which they did without hesitation.

I had just finished my questioning with the colonel when some of the more experienced prisoners took me to their room. They put me in a chair, gave me a cup of tea, and started to ask questions in the hundreds. They were especially interested to know when I thought the invasion would come, and when the war would be over. These were actually questions they knew more answers to than I. They seemed more abreast of the war than I was at this point. The only thing I could tell them was news local to Leuchars, the general mood and conditions in England, and what new aircraft had come on the scene since they were shot down. But in the grand scheme of things—the battlefields, the fronts, and so on—they knew much more than I did. Their walls were full of maps, and on these maps were red and blue lines—the frontlines. German newspapers arrived each day, and these had updates on what was going on, which the guys applied to their maps accordingly. We were dependant on the English news, and this was obviously the highlight of the day. News in English was also read outloud every morning. It was interesting to compare the German news to the English news. They did not always see eye to eye. If major events were unfolding, like the invasion of the continent, they were spread quickly by word of mouth and without pause for a public reading. When the invasion actually began, the reaction was interesting to observe. We had been waiting for so long for it to happen and so sure it would come that most of us just said, 'about bloody time.'

We were more than a little nervous that first week after the invasion, until a proper bridgehead had been secured in France. New prisoners came in, and they assured us that the Allies would not be pushed back towards the sea. It calmed us down considerably.

The date for the invasion had also been subject to much betting going around the camp. A couple of prisoners lost four years of income.

We had two radios in our camp, so if one was discovered and confiscated, we had one in reserve until we could replace the other. It was actually the German guards who got us the radios, which we traded for cigarettes. We had plenty of them (the cigarettes), and they had none. It usually started out with a small request about some kind of tool being brought to us from the outside. They got a few cigarettes for these small errands, which then escalated gradually until there was no way back for the German guards but to keep bringing the stuff in.

The camp was searched about once a week. About fifteen German soldiers came in and made a complete mess of our belongings. They seldom found anything of interest. If they did find a radio, they were extremely proud of themselves.

Receiving letters was a highlight. Erling and I were scared of writing home to our parents at first. We soon got in touch with other Norwegian prisoners in a neighbouring camp a few kilometres away, and asked them if they wrote letters home. We were told, much to our delight, that we could write as much as we wanted. I waited over two months before getting a reply to my first letter. When it finally came, it was such a relief. It made my life so much easier.

Jan Staubo

According to a letter dated 6 March 1944, it was Spitfire pilot Jan Staubo who told Eriksrud he could write as much as he wanted and in the Norwegian language. Staubo was transferred to Bellaria from another camp shortly before March 6th. In the same letter, Eriksrud introduces Erling Johanssen to his parents, and gives them Erling's address in Kristiansand. He recounts further on that he shares a room with Staubo, Johanssen, a Canadian, and five Englishmen. He mentions that they are all very nice chaps. Finn was aware of censorship and usually hesitant about saying anything negative at all; instead, he keeps his tone optimistic and tells of life in camp—sports, studies, and growing vegetables (see the collection of letters in the next chapter).

Not all letters were pleasant, though. A Canadian got a letter back from his family telling him they were so happy he had stayed in a camp that they had got both a swimming pool and a golf course. To put it mildly, we got very annoyed that people back home thought we had it so easy. In my honest opinion, the Germans basically treated their POWs as they should be treated, while the Allies treated theirs far too well.

I remember one English chap getting a letter from his wife telling him what a nice and handsome American she had met. The American would send him cigarettes soon, she wrote. Must be a rather uncomfortable letter to receive stuck in a prison camp.

From time to time we got packages that included clothes. Our families were allowed to send us four of these packages a year, with a maximum weight of 5 kg. Those of us of Norwegian descent got a near unlimited amount of packages because they conveniently travelled through German-occupied territory to get to us. They were never searched as thoroughly as the English and American packages, either.

I received many law books from home, and reading them gave me a lot of pleasure. I was also sent many books by the Swedish YMCA. They had an office in Sagan, and kept all the camps in the area equipped with different sporting goods, or simply helped us in any way they could. The Swedish YMCA became extremely popular with the prisoners, and we owe them so much. They were also allowed to visit us four to five times a year for a chat, and ask us in person what we wished for.

Representatives from neutral Switzerland also visited us every three months. We could complain to them if we felt we were not treated properly or didn't get the things we needed. The Germans usually promised they would meet our wishes and requirements, but it took a very long time for them to come through on their promises, if they did at all. It took six months until two proper showers were installed in the camp. Without those showers, the hot summers would have been unbearable. In the summer we could stay out longer, because of the daylight. During the winter, we were often closed in as soon as it got dark. There was also so much mud in the camp that simply walking around was a problem.

We spent the time in the camp as productively as we possibly could. There were two fairly good libraries. One with fiction, and one with non-fiction. We would sit there and read as much as we wanted. There were people with all kinds of professions in the camp, you could even learn Russian or Japanese if you wanted. I taught Norwegian myself. When we started out, I had twenty eager students at my disposal; after a couple of weeks, there were five left. I am not sure if this was because of the teacher or the language. Only two of my students made it through the entire course, but it paid off, for they spoke pretty passable Norwegian when the war ended.

Most prisoners usually spent most of their time in their bunks with a book. With twelve men to one little room, the bunk was the only free space we had. If you had the bottom bunk, you could be in for both kicks and punches during the night. After one winter we knew each other remarkably well, perhaps a little too well. We always found things that annoyed us silly with each other, things we would never think twice of in normal life. It was inevitable that we got on each other nerves. Erling and I had been lucky with our roommates. They were all quiet and calm sorts of chaps, who never bothered much with arguments. They usually kept to themselves and didn't give any trouble. All of them went through the blues, though. One of the guys stayed in his bunk for a couple of days without moving so much as a finger. He didn't eat much, and he didn't say anything. Just stayed there looking at the ceiling.

The food was decent enough, but only thanks to the Red Cross parcels. What we got from the Germans didn't do much for us—some potatoes and a thin soup. The first six months I was there, we got a Red Cross parcel each week. Those of us who were Norwegian also got a second parcel from the Norwegian Red Cross each month, and four Danish ones a year. The Norwegian one contained typical Norwegian fare like goat's cheese. The Englishmen were so thrilled about this cheese I had to promise to send them this stuff when the war was over.

We made our own food, and each barracks had a cooking team. We usually alternated who the dedicated chef would be, but some of us found being the chef so exciting that they kept at the job all year around. They thought that cooking was a lot of fun, and it helped the time pass quickly, too. They became true champions of cooking, and it was amazing what they managed to come up with with these Red Cross parcels we got. For Christmas, they made what looked like posh London cakes of the finest sort.

Our Christmas meal consisted of five courses, two of which were the chicken and plum-pudding from American parcels. Drink, on the other hand, was a rare occurrence in the camp. Some people tried making wine out of raisins and sugar. The result was very strong. In the end it was forbidden to explore it further, since we had to live on half the usual number of packages for the last six months of our stay. We would rather eat the raisins than drink them, anyway. The wine went by the name of 'Kriegibru'.

Speaking of words and languages, a whole new sort of language developed between the prisoners. Some words entered daily usage, and could have several different meanings. Here's a small selection of them:

Kriegi: prisoner of war (minimum of six months' stay in Germany).
Goon: German.
Ferret: German guard doing favours.
Pit: Bunk.
Pitbashing: Lying in the bunk.
Cooler: Cell.
Dhobi: Wash.
Gash: Surplus (of food).
Stooge: The cook's assistant.
Griff: News.
Dugg gen: Unreliable news.
Round the bend: Crazy.
To shoot a line: Brag.

Bunks in Stalag Luft III. (*Finn Eriksrud's collection*)

19

Tunnelling

There is one thing that a prisoner thinks about constantly: how to escape. The most common method for us was to dig tunnels. If you got really desperate, you could perhaps try to climb over the fence. Men got out of the camp in the most bizarre ways imaginable. One day, twenty-nine British officers got out the main gate right before the German guards' eyes. There had been an insect infestation in one of the barracks, and the Germans had given permission for twenty-five of us to be cleansed of them a day. This had been going on for some time, so the guards had got used to seeing twenty-five of us march out of the main gate. So, just after a change of guard one day, twenty-five guys lined up with a blanket under their arms. Four chaps with good German language skills and dressed in German uniforms made inside the camp played the part as guards. They screamed and shouted orders in the German way, and when they reached the main gate they showed the real guards their fake papers and everyone simply marched out. Just around the first bend, they disappeared in all directions. Half an hour later, the Germans discovered what had been going on. They were all recaptured, and as punishment for their crime got fourteen days in the cooler on nothing but water and bread, and without cigarettes or books either.

It was common for groups or single individuals to plan escape attempts. It was an unwritten law that if you had a good idea for escape and were likely to be successful, others would do what they could to help you.

When it came to tunnels, however, there was so much work involved that the entire camp had to be in on it. The digging itself weren't the biggest issue. It was usually just three or four guys doing it. The most important part was having a good emergency system in place when a German guard came too close. For this you needed many of us, and good organisation. If the Germans got suspicious of our activities, we had to act fast and efficiently. The biggest problem with the tunnels was how to get rid of all the sand and dirt. Usually, this was taken care of by each of us having our own little pocket inside our trousers, which was filled with sand. We would then go for a stroll around the camp. While we were walking, we pulled on a small cord connected to the bag so it gradually let loose all the sand. All this digging required patience, but we had time at our disposal.

More than often, those who wanted out of the camp did get out, but very few of us made the home run all the way back to England. Most of us were caught quickly, though some managed to stay outside for months. A Czech pilot in the camp had been a prisoner for four whole years, but had not spent more than one and a half years in the camp itself. He usually stayed in his home country, and twice got to the Swiss border, though didn't manage to cross it. In the end the Germans got sick of his antics. When they caught him for the third time they sent him to some punitive camp, specially made for those who offended again and again. Life there was much stricter, letters and parcels being sparse. When the Germans threatened one of us with that stuff the next time he was captured, he usually kept his head down for a while.

The Gestapo usually did not get involved here, but obviously did in the much talked about escape from the north camp, a few kilometres away from us. Two Norwegians managed to make their way back to England. Two other Norwegians were murdered by the Gestapo upon recapture.

Another sport we got ourselves involved in was stealing from the German guards. After one barracks inspection, the Germans left short of two of their flashlights and a small tool.

There were other events and situations which were more pleasant. One day, a German SS colonel came to the camp. He was stupid enough to park his shiny car on our 'sports ground'. When he left the car, all the prisoners came rushing over to it and completely surrounded it. The driver got as many cigarettes as he wanted, while everyone walked around the car admiring how nice it looked. While this went on, the prisoners took anything remotely possible from it. It was a miracle the car even started when the colonel left the camp. After a short while, we got a message from the colonel that we could keep everything we had nicked from it, as long as he got his travel documents back, so he could actually leave the area—he had left his precious documents in the car in a bag. The eldest among us brought the subject up for discussion and decided to give the documents back to him, which we couldn't do much with anyway. We stamped them with 'approved' in any case, just as the Germans did with books that arrived in the camp. The documents were also signed by Winston Churchill while they went 'missing'.

Until we got the news of the murder of those fifty escapees from the north camp, the whole escape business had been a sport to us. But the situation changed dramatically after that, and we started to think twice about escaping. The English colonel advised us to cool our heels, since the price we would have to pay for was too big. Later on, a message came from the Germans that didn't make escaping any easier. Parts of Germany were considered strictly off-limits, since we would be shot on sight if we got too close. We felt a little frightened by it all.

Norwegians in the Great Escape

Finn Eriksrud did not take part in the famous escape, since he was located in another camp. However, news travelled about the murders. Four Norwegian pilots did participate in this escape: Per Bergsland, Jens Müller, Haldor Espelid, and Nils Jørgen Fuglesang. The following scenes are drawn from Cato Guhnfeldt and Simon Read's research on the subject, and which appeared in *Spitfire Saga V* (2014) and *Human Game: Hunting the Great Escape Murderers* (2013).

Espelid and Fuglesang decided to stick together during their escape. They headed for Berlin, so their forged documents must have been checked several times and found to be acceptable. They made it as far as Flensburg before they were caught. The two friends were walking down a street, perhaps thinking of ways to cross the Danish border, when the police noticed them. They were questioned, and admitted they were escapees. Neither of them seemed to take it very seriously or fear any grave repercussions. In the past, caught prisoners were given a month or so in a single cell. But the Norwegians were unaware of Hitler's latest command to shoot the fifty of them. No one was. Espelid and Fuglesang confirmed they had been travelling by train before being caught. SS Sturmbannführer Johannes Post was second-in-command of the Gestapo in Kiel, Germany. On 29 March 1944, he was sent to Flensburg to murder those escapees who had been caught in this area. Besides the two Norwegians, another two were caught in North Germany: James Catanach from Australia, and Arnold Christensen from New Zealand. The four of them were picked up at the police station in Flensburg by Post and another Gestapo officer, Franz Schmidt. They brought two drivers with them to take turns on guard duty, and left Flensburg with the four prisoners in two separate cars, Schmidt driving the other. Just outside the city, Post ordered the driver to stop and told Catanach to get out and relieve himself, as it would be a long drive. As the Catanach left the car and walked a few metres onto a nearby field to do so, Post walked up behind him and shot him in the back. Catanach instantly fell to the ground, dead. Moments later, the second car came to the scene with the three other prisoners, who were let out to stretch their legs much like Catanach. But they quickly spotted his lifeless body, and realising what had happened, tried to make a run for it. They were immediately shot, two of them dying instantly. One of the three prisoners was still alive, and tried to speak. Post walked up to him and shot him in the head.

After the war, Post said he had informed the prisoners of what was coming so they could make amends with God. The RAF later launched a search for Johannes Post which lasted two years. He was caught hiding in the apartment of a lover under a false name. During the subsequent trial, one of the drivers involved told the court that it was Post who had been the most active, and that he seemed to enjoy murdering the pilots. In his defence, Post argued that he would have been a poor national-socialist had he not carried out a direct order, regardless of whether the prisoners' lives were supposed to be protected by the Geneva Convention. Johannes Post was found guilty and hanged. Of all those involved in and convicted of the murder of the RAF escapees, three had a direct hand in the murder of Fuglesang and Espelid.

Only three of the seventy-three participants in the Great Escape survived. Jens Müller and Per Bergsland were the other Norwegians who had paired up. They were the forty-third and forty-fourth to emerge from tunnel 'Harry', the ease of which Müller was surprised by—it took him just three minutes to get through it. After getting out, they rearranged their clothes and walked to the Sagan railway station. Bergsland was wearing a civilian suit he had made for himself from a Royal Marine uniform, and an RAF overcoat only slightly altered with brown leather sewn over the buttons. He also wore a black RAF tie, but no hat, and carried a small suitcase sent to him from Norway, just like Espelid and Fuglesang had. In it he had Norwegian toothpaste and soap, sandwiches, and 164 Reichsmarks given to him by the escape committee.

The pair took the 2.04 a.m. train to Frankfurt-an-der-Oder. Their papers stated they were Norwegian electricians from the *Arbeitslager* there and working in the vicinity of Sagan. Then onwards to Stettin, for which they had other papers attesting a different place of work. They travelled in a third-class carriage with ordinary civilians, and looked the part. They arrived at Frankfurt at 6.00 a.m. and caught a connecting train to Küstrin. They settled in a cafeteria, and were quickly approached by a police officer asking for documents. The German studied them closely, looked at the two Norwegians, then said everything was in order, saluted them, and left. They had got away with it! They then took the 10.00 a.m. train from Küstrin to Stettin and arrived around lunchtime.

In Stettin they got in touch with Swedish fishermen via an address given to them by the escape committee. It was in fact a brothel for foreigners, where no Germans were allowed. The Swede they were able to contact there agreed to smuggle them aboard his ship and take them to Sweden. They came with him down to the harbour, and were to wait for his signal to come aboard—but no signal came, and the ship left the dock without them. They got a room at a nearby hotel and went to sleep. The next day they decided to visit the brothel again to seek out more Swedish sailors. They got in touch with a couple of Swedes who agreed to their plan, and whom they followed down to the harbour, once again. A German guard checked the Swedes' papers, and let the Norwegians pass when the sailors said they were all part of the same crew.

A German inspection was expected before departure the next day, and the two Norwegians had to hide below deck. They found cover in the anchor locker, in one corner of which there was a pile of netting and sacks. They sailors pulled it aside and formed a nest.

The next day they waited while a German soldier inspected the boat. In an interview in the mid-1990s, Müller recounts how the German had let his hand run from the Norwegian's shoulder all the way down to his waist without noticing that it was a person he was touching. He then gave up the search, and left. Müller and Bergsland sailed to Sweden, and with the help of the British Embassy travelled back to England. Bergsland passed away in 1992, and Müller in 1999.

But despite the sombre news of the murders, we didn't completely renounce our tunnelling efforts. We had to keep up the appearance of escaping. Not many of us were very keen on making a run for it any longer, though. Goebbels had got involved as well, and said he could not guarantee any *Terrorflieger*'s safety if he was shot down over Germany. The civilian population was encouraged to attack pilots they found by any means they deemed fit.

But despite all these goings-on, life in the camp became boring and monotonous. Each day was just like another, and it was hard to separate them.

Every afternoon, if the weather permitted, Erling and I would go for our routine stroll around camp. It took us exactly four and a half minutes. We had to do several circuits in order to get a proper walk out of it. There weren't many things left that we hadn't touched on while walking, so we sometimes struggled to make conversation. Little bits and pieces of daily life were missing here, so topics were few and far between. We did discuss when we thought the war would end though. If we got good news about the progress of the war, our spirits rose quickly and many would predict it would be over within months. If bad news reached us, apathy rapidly crept over the camp. Our only comfort was the knowledge that it had to end at some point.

The winter of 1945 came upon us, and we didn't much relish receiving only half the amount of parcels we had got in the summer. However, the Russians started their offensive around this time and shortly reached Oder. Seemingly endless streams of refugees started to pass the camp. There were few men, just women and children.

20

Final Victory

We could soon hear artillery fire from the frontlines. We knew our time at the camp was coming to an end, but when?

One evening, 200 English pilots came in to camp. They had marched 200 km in -20-degree temperature, without food or sleep. They were in a terrible condition, and we started to worry about what would happen to us if we were forced to move. We prepared as best as we could—our boots and backpacks—and hoped that the Russians would hurry up. Not long after the Englishmen arrived, we heard the Russians had gained control of a bridgehead over the Oder. We hoped they would reach Sagan before the Germans could make their move on us.

The Germans did not react for a while longer, so we thought they had given up on the task of moving 10,000 men. We all sighed with relief and patiently waited for our rescue.

While we were playing bridge one evening at the end of January, the order came for us to march out of camp within half an hour. The English colonel protested, and was of the absolutely correct opinion that it was madness to send 10,000 men out into the bitter cold. The Germans ignored him, and the only thing he could do was postpone the march for another half hour. So in the end we got an hour to prepare, and the camp erupted into frantic activity. We made swift work of small sledges using tables, boxes, and other materials. Everything that could slide on ice or snow was packed, from pots and pans to rocking chairs, besides which we only brought the most essential items, such as blankets, food, and cigarettes. At around 1 o'clock in the morning, we left the camp.

By the gate we all got a Red Cross parcel each. Food-wise, we got one fifth of a bread roll each, and this was supposed to last us five days. Many of us had been smart and brought lots of cigarettes, with which you could buy bread. At first, one bread roll was valued at sixty to seventy cigarettes, but after a while bread became scarce and the price went up to 200 cigarettes.

The best trade I ever heard of on this march was an American's, who traded twenty cigarettes and a can of cheese for a horse and a cart. We weren't the only refugees out on the roads walking, but it was only when we reached cities that we saw the German refugees, as we always had to march on small village roads away from everyone else. We marched around 80 km in a week. We couldn't really complain about marching by day; at night we would find shelter in barns. The atmosphere among us was pretty good, all things considered, despite a few injuries. The news from the front was good, and rumours circulated wildly. We expected the Russians to catch up with us at any time. In reality, the Russians had halted at Oder and hadn't moved forward (for a short while).

When we got to Spremberg we boarded a train to Luckenwalde, about 50 km south of Berlin. This was a large camp holding about 15 to 20,000 prisoners of all nationalities—Americans, Italians, Norwegians, Englishmen, Russians, Poles, Frenchmen, and so on. Each nation was separated by barb-wired fences.

We arrived there in the evening, and when I awoke the next morning, I was shocked to have an Englishman come over and tell me there were about 1,150 Norwegian prisoners on the other side of the fence I was looking at. It turned out that these were officers evacuated from Schildberg. Gen. Otto Ruge was there as well, and he made an arrangement with the Germans to move us Norwegians who had arrived from Bellaria into their camp. It took a few months for this to happen, though.

General Otto Ruge

Otto Ruge was most widely known as the Chief of Defence (CHOD) during the invasion Norway in April to June 1940. He was born in Kristiania (Oslo) on 9 January 1882 and became an officer at the age of 20. Gen. Kristian Laake left his position as CHOD over disagreement on the response to the German attack on 9 April 1940, and the next day Ruge was promoted to Major-General. He was then promoted to CHOD on 18 May 1940, taking charge of Norway's chaotic defensive strategy and making tough decisions amid the inertia of his fellow officers, even ordering the removal of officers who did put up a fight. His plan of action ultimately failed in the face of overwhelming odds; the Allies' help turned out to be too weak to push back the invading forces. He was imprisoned in Germany for refusing to sign an agreement not to take up arms against the Reich again.

Gen. Ruge remained in captivity for the reminder of the war. He took up his position as CHOD again in the summer of 1945, but left six months later because he was unable to see eye-to-eye with the Minister of Defence, Jens Christian Hauge. He passed away on 15 August 1961.

We did not get off to a good start in Luckenwalde. We had no Red Cross parcels, so had to live off German rations. We got considerably thinner. All conversation turned to food. What to eat now, and what to eat when we came back home. We had no books, either, so times were rough. The Norwegian officers eventually began to receive Swedish, Danish, and Norwegian parcels. They were generous and shared these with the English and American prisoners, but it was far from enough to feed us all.

The Danes were outstanding at bringing parcels in. It became impossible to send them by train, so they drove them down to Luckenwalde in trucks for as long it was possible to use German roads.

The only highlight at Luckenwalde was access to English news, given to us daily. We had brought our radio from Sagan. The Norwegian officers had lost one of their radios when they had arrived, but later bought it back from the same people who had taken it for 2,000 cigarettes.

Those who lived under the absolute worst conditions were the Russians. They got no parcels, as they did not have a treaty with the Red Cross. We asked the Germans if the Russians could be given some of ours, but they declined. Not only that, but they also went to the Russians and told them that *they* had asked if *we* wanted to give them some of our parcels, but had refused.

I saw a few Norwegian newspapers down here, and in one of them I read an article about our exit from Sagan. According to the newspaper, we had begged the Germans to go west so as not to fall into in Russian hands. Apparently, when we were told that this was hard to do, but could be done, we were supposed to have shouted hoorays. None of this was true of course, but there was lots of dangerous propaganda going about which could make cooperation between the Allies harder.

There were POWs from so many nations at Luckenwalde. They all had fantastic stories to share, especially the pilots. A Canadian navigator told me how he had jumped out the bomber with no parachute over Berlin from 1,000 feet up. As incredible as it sounds, he only broke his legs. He's still alive and well. This was during the winter, and he fell straight into a large pile of snow, plus the speed of his fall was dramatically reduced by several large trees before he landed. He's still alive and well.

There were hundreds of stories going around about the amazing ways in which pilots had been rescued, but I think the story about the falling Canadian beats them all. If I hadn't heard it straight from the guy himself, I wouldn't have believed it.

As spring of 1945 came upon us, we started to look at life through a brighter lens. The parcels arrived, the English forces were getting closer, and so were the Americans and the Russians. It was exciting to ask ourselves who would reach us first, and as always, bets were placed. During the night we heard artillery fire from the south-east, and we figured it to be Russian.

One day, we were in our usual morning detention, and the German commander was doing what he always did. Suddenly, he simply left with a group of German guards, leaving behind only a few on fence duty. When they weren't relieved by new guards, they realised what was going on. They became very offended, and didn't really know what to do. One of them sold his rifle to a prisoner for ten cigarettes, and then disappeared. Soon, all of them had vanished, and we took charge of the camp. The camp's command consisted of Gen. Otto Ruge, an English colonel, and an American colonel. We hung up white sheets on the fence surrounding us, and quickly sent the rest of our parcels to the Russians.

It was another 24 hours before the Russians finally arrived. On the 21st of April, five Russian tanks entered the camp and tore down the barbed wire.

Freedom had finally come.

Erling Victor Johanssen's escape

Erling recounts the story of his escape in the local Kristiansand newspaper on 12 October 1998. Both he and Eriksrud decided to escape from Luckenwalde while the Russians were approaching from the east and the Americans from the west. They headed west and were one day stopped by an American jeep full of smiling American soldiers, who took care of them and sent them to Belgium. From there they were sent back to London and eventually returned to Norway in June 1945. Eriksrud does not mention any of this and it's possible that the journalist embellished Erling's account. After arriving back in Norway, he took up a job as a telegraphist with Det Norske Luftselskap (the predecessor of Scandinavian Airlines). He also studied French in his spare time, already being able to speak English and German fluently after his adventures in Canada, Britain, and Germany. This was contributing factor in his promotion to a Scandinavian Airlines representative at Cointrin Airport in Geneva, where he stayed for a year. There he met a Danish girl, whom he fell in love and moved to Copenhagen with. He started to work in his father-in-law's clothing factory, but soon left to start his own business, delivering naval equipment to the Danish military, the fishing industry, and shipping companies. The move paid off, and he started two more businesses shortly thereafter. His last business took him to the electronics industry, in which he employed at least seventy-five people full-time. While he was making a success of his career, he was less fortunate in his personal life. His first wife died after only ten years of marriage, and he re-married, only to see his second wife, Hanna, die of a serious illness merely seven years later. Erling was exhausted by these ordeals, and sold his companies in order to retire to a more quiet life. He attended Finn's seventieth birthday in 1992, the same year as Hanna's death, and celebrated his own, eightieth birthday in 1998. Erling Victor Johanssen died on 13 November 2006, and is buried in his hometown of Kristiansand. He had no children.

Thor Heisten, Alex Vercoe, and Erling Victor Johanssen in London during the war. They were all from the same town, Kristiansand, in Norway. (*Erling Johanssen's collection*)

Finn Eriksrud after the war

Finn contemplated becoming a full-time pilot after the war, which many of the other veterans did. He kept at it for some time after the hostilities ended, and was stationed at Sola, Stavanger, flying Mosquitos in the summertime. A horrific incident involving a Mosquito's wing breaking off in mid-air may have been the cause for Finn to take up a job in education instead—the pilot had been killed in the accident.

Eriksrud decided to re-launch his law studies upon return to Norway. However, during the summer of 1945, he met publisher Ernst G. Mortensen on Oslo's high street. Mortensen was very eager back then, and one of the first in his field to spot the potential of war memoirs. Eriksrud was already acquainted with Mortensen, and was talked into writing about his wartime experiences. The book came out the following autumn, and a total of 5,000 copies were produced. Eriksrud used the income to support himself through university. After graduating, he started working in his father's law firm, Hiorth-Eriksrud. He married and had three children, and worked as a lawyer until he retired in the mid-1990s.

Finn Eriksrud passed away in 2004. His younger sister, Rikke, is still alive and well.

Above left: Finn Eriksrud, safely back in Norway, enjoying his pipe on a summer day. (*Finn Eriksrud's collection*)

Above right: Finn Eriksrud, most likely flying an Airspeed Oxford over Norway. (*Finn Eriksrud's collection*)

Appendix:
Letters Home

3/2—1944

Dear father and mother: I am a prisoner of war in Germany. I am fit and well, hope you are too. I am in a camp with British officers, and have everything I need. I would like to continue to study law. Can you send me the necessary books? I am sorry to tell you that Gunnar is killed. I will write you more later. Give my regards to all my friends. Your affectionate son. Finn.

6/3—1944

Dear father, mother, Emil and Rikke!
I guess you will have already received a card from me by the time you get this. I wrote it in English, because I thought it would reach you quicker, but Jan Staubo, transferred here from another camp the other day, tells me that it doesn't matter what language I write in. Besides Jan there is another Norwegian here, my navigator, a very pleasant chap from Kristiansand. His name is Erling Victor Johanssen. His family lives in Prost Larssens Gt 8, Kristiansand S. We are both in good shape, healthy and well. Since I last saw you [in Norway] I have only spent one day in bed, and this was after vaccination. I hope you will receive this letter before mother's birthday on the 16th, and I wish her a happy birthday, and hope we can meet again before the next. I'm having a good time here. I am living together with Jan, Erling, a Canadian, and five Englishmen. They are all very polite, top guys. Two of them are very interested in learning Norwegian, and I teach them for an hour each day. They would like to write to Norwegians, so if you like, would you give me the address of someone who would be interested? Jan brought with him plenty of Norwegian books, one on economics among them, so I have started to read it. I hope you can send me some law books. In the meantime I am reading English law. Otherwise I have got everything I need. I will write to you again soon. I hope everything is fine

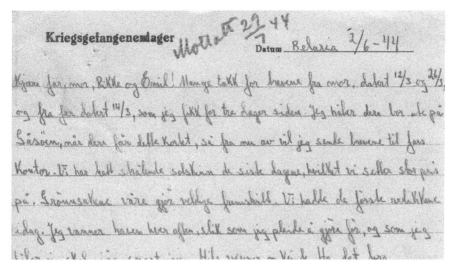

One of the letters Finn Eriksrud wrote to his parents as a POW. (*Finn Eriksrud's collection*)

with all of you. I am eagerly awaiting letters and photographs from you back home. My regards to friends and acquaintances.

Much love from Finn.

15/3—1944

Dear Rikke! The time is about 22:00, we have just had an evening meal, done the dishes, and I have lit my pipe which arrived in a parcel together with another from the Norwegian Red Cross. Believe me when I say I was pleased when I got them. Many thanks to all of you. I am waiting for letters from you every day now. I also hope you write to me, and also send a photograph, as I am sure you have changed since the last time I saw you. We make time pass by to the best of our ability here. We get up around nine in the morning. Actually, Bill, an Englishman, gets up around 8.30 and serves the rest of us a cup of tea in bed. At ten there's a 'rollcall', and most of us have managed to get up by then. Then we eat breakfast, peel potatoes and clean our room. The time until lunch, which we have at around one o' clock, I spend studying law. It is a great relief to study it in Norwegian using books I already know. After lunch I teach two of the Englishmen in my room Norwegian. They are very eager to learn, and I think they learned a lot in a fairly short while. We eat dinner around five, and it is not so bad. I will tell you later what the English, Canadian and American Red Cross packages contain. I did not believe my eyes when I saw what I got from Norway. Crisp bread and goat's cheese. It's amazing. I will continue to tell what we're doing in my next letter. It is mother's birthday tomorrow. I hope she has a lovely day. Say hello to mother, father, Emil and everyone I know. Take care, bye bye. Much love from Finn.

Sagan 28/3—44

Dear Emil! I was very happy to receive your letter today. It is perhaps a bit difficult for you to understand how much we appreciate getting these letters. It is truly the highlight of the day when the letters are brought to us, and you might understand how happy I was to hear from you, the first letter I have received so far, but I hope there will be more on a regular basis now. Perhaps you can send some photographs as well. I think you should be very pleased with your mid-term grades. I am very impressed with the result in Norwegian language. I bet a piece of chocolate with Jan Staubo that I would get a letter today. When Jan received a package from England which, among other things, contained chocolate, I became one chocolate bar richer. You have to tell me how the skiing season has been this year. How was it at Vestenden, and who you were with *etc.* I find it a bit hard so far to sit down and study, but I do read 3–4 hours a day (economy and law). It is hard to exercise here, there's mud everywhere, but we're out c. two hours a day when it is not raining too much. Have you been out at Gåsøen [a small island in the Oslofjord] yet? I met the Boy Scout leader and his wife just before I was shot down. He's doing fine. How are both the Jans doing? You have to tell them to write me. My regards to father, mother, Rikke and the rest of the family. Take care, and bye bye. Much love from Finn.

Sagan 3/4—44

Dear mother and father! I have just received the letter mother wrote on the 5th of March. I got a letter from Jan G. at the same time. He gave me no return address, could you send it to me, because I would like to write him. I was also very happy to hear that you have sent me toiletries, many thanks. Otherwise I have everything I need, but if you perhaps could send me 'FROM BUSINESS AND POLITICS' by Sindeng and 'STATISTICAL YEARBOOK', doesn't matter the year of publishing. Today I spent two hours digging up a small piece of land, where we will be able to grow vegetables in a few weeks' time. Each room gets a small piece of land to grow veggies on. About a week ago we had a theatre play. We also have an orchestra consisting of 15–16 men. They play from time to time. All the members are prisoners of war, and they are playing very well. Some of them have 3–4 years' experience, so they have picked up a few things along the way. Before I was shot down, I met Inger T. She is happily married, and is doing just fine. Gunnar H. and I had lunch with her, and we had a nice chat about the good old days. It was the last time I saw Gunnar. I assume Rikke will have had her birthday by the time you get this letter. You must congratulate her from me. My regards to the family and all friends, and tell them that letters and photographs are most welcome. Take care, much love from Finn.

6/4—44

Dear mother. Today I got the first letter you sent me, dated the 23rd of February. I am very happy that you are all healthy and well. I am in good health myself. You wouldn't believe how fun it is to read law again, especially in Norwegian. You have to thank Per and the Jans [Finns friends back in Norway, Per Borge, Jan Friis, and Jan Getz] for the presents. I also have plenty of time to read novels. There's a library here, so there's plenty of reading material. My regards to Emil, Rikke and the family. Take care! Much love from Finn.

Sagan 20/4—1944

Dear father, mother, Emil and Rikke. It's been a while since I have heard from you now. I hope you are well and healthy and doing fine. I received the Red Cross parcel a couple of days ago. It was good to taste goat's cheese again. I have already taken orders from my roommates for goat's cheese after the war.

[At this point 5 lines have been completely blacked out—either censorship, or Finn deciding to re-write his letter.]

We have had wonderful spring weather lately. We have grown radishes, carrots, tomatoes and a few other types on our small piece of land. We have also got the footballs out, and we're playing a match each day. It was wonderful to run around and get warm and then take a cold shower afterwards. The other day we had a small gramophone concert. We played Per Gynt for example, and I appreciated listening to Norwegian music again so much. The law studies are slowly coming along. Jan Staubo has started studying Russian, and I think his progress is even slower than mine in law. Do wish father happy birthday, if you should be getting this letter before the 28th of May. Bye bye. Much love from Finn.

27/4—44

Dear father, mother, Emil and Rikke. Today I have been what we call 'a lucky kriegi'. Yesterday afternoon I received several Norwegian books about law.

Today I received a package with shaving equipment, and then later on in the very same day got two envelopes with photographs of father and 'Gåsehuset' [family hut on the island of Gåsøya]. It is hard to say what pleases me the most, but I am sure that the biggest surprise was the photo of Emil. Most people here figured he was around 20–25 years old, and they were rather shocked when I told them he had just turned 18. Rikke has also changed greatly, and people were astonished that I had a sister who looks 'so sweet', as well as a mother who 'looks so young'. Together with the photo of father they are now hanging over my bed. There are no excuses not to study now. I have all the books I need for a good while ahead. We have a room which is only used for studying, so there are no difficulties finding peace and quiet. You do not have to send me more toiletries, as I have all I need and everything else. In a month today I should also be getting a uniform package from England. Many thanks for everything. Take care. From Finn.

Bellaria 10/5—44

Dear aunt Ellen and uncle Emil. Many thanks for your letter, dated the 12th of April. I got it yesterday. I have not received the last letter yet, but I am sure it will pop up soon. It is nice to hear that everything is well with the children and yourselves. I am doing just fine. We've started spring preparations just like you. About a month ago we sowed radishes, carrots and tomatoes. We've been given 1.5 to 3.0 sq m of earth. It's been rather chilly the past month, so we have not yet seen any results. The radishes are the only ones to arrive so far, and as usual they were sowed too close to each other. We've had to thin it out considerably. 'Bill', or 'uncle William' as we call him, is our garden master. He's 38 years old, and has been in the RAF for about 20 years. He hopes to retire after the war, and get a decent enough income so he can live off it. With the money he's saved up being a prisoner of war (he's been here for three years) he wants to buy a motorboat, and together with his wife (he hasn't told her anything about his plans yet) he wants to travel around the rivers and lakes of Europe. He's wondering if he should send her on a navigational course, so he can be in charge of cooking. My regards to little Ellen and Eli, and say happy birthday to them. My regards also to Eva and the rest of the family. Take care. Much love from Finn.

Bellaria 11/5—44

Dear father, mother, Emil and Rikke. Many thanks for your letters. Received from mother; 2/4, 9/4 and 11/4. From father; 23/2, 3/4, 14/4 and 14/4. From

Emil 14/4. I have also received the toiletries and the photographs. I appreciate both greatly, especially the photographs. We can only write three letters and four cards in one month. I have also received a letter from Morten in Kragerø [a Norwegian town]. Please thank him from me when you can. We are doing just fine, and got everything we need. We've had beautiful weather these last few days, and we're doing plenty of sport. Take care and say hello to all friends and acquaintances. From Jan, from Erling. Much love, from Finn. [Jan Staubo and Erling Johanssen both signed this card]

Bellaria 28/5—44

Dear Rikke!
Many thanks for your letter dated 23/4 which I received the other day. I planned to write a card to congratulate father with his birthday, but I forgot. I hope you will do it for me. Could you also thank Olav Foss for his letter, dated 31/3 which I also received a short while ago. This afternoon, I was at a theatre play in the camp. The play was called 'Arsenic and old lace'. It was written by an American shortly after the war started, and it was a major success in both New York and London. It was welcomed with great applause here too. There are many good actors in the camp; personally I do not really understand just how they can achieve such great results. During the breaks, the orchestra played dance music. They have also made great progress in the later months, and is very popular with 'The Kriegies'. Yesterday we had dried and salted cod for dinner. Even the English had to admit it wasn't too bad. It's beautiful sunshine today we've spent most of the time out in the sun. I am very excited about what you and Emil will do for your exams. I have the books I need for now. We have received two books about economy from the Swedish KFUM. I would very much like those books I mentioned the other day. Otherwise, we're doing quite well, and time is running fairly quick. You have to say hello to father, mother, Emil and the rest of the family, as well as friends and acquaintances. Take care, much love from Finn. Hilsen Jan. [Jan Staubo yet again signed one of Finns letters in the bottom left corner].

Bellaria 2/6—44

Dear father, mother, Rikke and Emil! Many thanks for the letters from mother, dated 12/3 and 26/3 and from father 14/3. I recieved them three days ago. I hope you are living out at Gåsøen [island] when you recieve this letter, so from now on I will send the letters to fathers office. We've had brilliant sunshine here the past days, which we all appreciated. Our vegetables are making good progress. We had the first redish today. I am watering the small garden each evening, as I used to do before.. *[the scanner sadly did not scan the last sentence completely]*. Say hello to friends. Take care. Much love from Finn.

Bellaria 5/6—44

Dear father, mother, Rikke and Emil. Many thanks for the letter from mother, dated 12/3, 26/3 and from father dated 14/3 which I recieved a week ago. All is well here, and I hope you are doing well and are all healthy. I am very excited about Rikke and Emil's exams. Did they make it? The other day we had a spring clean of our room. We got up early, around 8, and took everything that could be moved out the window. Then we went to work on the floor, the walls and the ceiling with our brushes and warm soapy water. It was incredible to observe all the dust and dirt which had gathered during the winter. We got most of it. We also cleaned the doors, the lockers, the tables and the chairs. So, our room is pretty clean at the moment. The cooking job is shared among us, and each of us is cook for one month at a time. This month it's my turn. I rather like it, because it lets me off anything else that needs to be done—for example doing the dishes. The only hot meal we cook is dinner for the evening. In those Red Cross parcels we get each week, there's canned meat, raisins or prunes, biscuits, butter, jam, cheese, powdered milk, sugar, coffee or tea. We get these parcels from England, Canada, the USA, and we, the Norwegians, also get parcels from Norway and Denmark. We're not suffering in any way. I just wish I could send you something in return. As you also understand, you don't have to send me more food, since if it takes a toll on your own rations back home. My law studies are slowly progressing. Say hello to our family and friends. Jan also sends his greetings. Take care, much love from Finn.

[From this date and onwards, Finn no longer writes the name of the camp on his letters back home.]

12/6—44

Dear father, mother, Rikke and Emil. Many thanks for the letter from mother dated 7/5, from Bibi 7/5, Paul 6/5. I am happy to hear that Emil did very well on his exams. I guess we will be starting serious law studies together, at the same time. I guess I will have to take those pre-exams once more. Life goes on much as usual over here, everyone is well and healthy. We're all pretty restless hearing of the latest happenings on the west coast. Say hello to the rest of the

family and our friends. Much love from Finn.
28/6—44

Dear father, mother, Emil and Rikke! Many thanks for your letters from father, dated 4/5, and 26/5. From mother 24/5 and 30/5, from Emil 4/6. Also from Uncle Emil dated 23/5 and 4/5, from Uncle Edvard 19/4 and Dordi 20/4. From Jan Getz 29/4, from Bibi 6/5, from Greta Rydtun 23/5 and from Gammelvegens Boghandel 23/5. This letter contained only of one piece of paper giving details about economy for the law exam. I am assuming that those books sent at the same time have arrived, and I will be receiving them as soon as they have been through censorship. Otherwise, I have been getting everything you've sent me so far. About getting parcels from the Norwegian Embassy in Paris, I think recent events makes this hard. Jan wrote to Paris about 2 months ago on this subject, so far without result, so I think it best to wait and see before doing anything else. It is sad to hear that mother has not been feeling well lately, but a relief to hear she's doing better now. I truly hope that both she and the rest of you are in good health. It was very nice to receive the photographs from Uncle Emil, and hear that everything is going well. I am also very excited to hear about Emil and Rikke's final exam grades. I have not heard from Lall yet, but I will write her a letter this afternoon. I will also write to all of my different contacts as long as I have cards left. In the meantime, take care. Jan sends his greetings. Much love, from Finn.

7/7—43 [Finn wrote the date wrong, for he was not in captivity as early as this—he most likely means July 1944. This error was perhaps symptomatic of camp life's repetitiveness.]

Dear father, mother, Emil and Rikke. Many thanks for the letter from mother, dated May 18th. In June I got a total of 21 letters, so you I'm sure you understand my elevated spirits. We've had a great month, beautiful warm weather. We're all nice and tanned, in great moods, all healthy and well. We're eating salads three times a day, and we still have enough to last for a long time. You must say hello to the rest of the family, and our friends. Take care. Greetings from Jan, much love from Finn.

Bellaria 10/7—43 [Finn wrote the date wrong, as he was not in captivity on the 10th of July 1943.]

Dear father, mother, Emil and Rikke. It finally started to rain again today. It is nice, for a change, to see the rain pouring down. Our garden needed it, even if we water it every afternoon. We've already had much joy from what we sewed in the spring, but we do lack good soil. Every time a horse comes into our camp, 'kriegies' follow it around with cardboard boxes in their hands and hopeful expressions on their faces. If by chance the horse should do us a favour, there is great cheering from the 'kriegies.' Then we march back to our respective gardens with the catch of the day. If I'm not mistaken, this was something we also did at Gåsøen. I can remember that I was once sent out with a bucket to try my luck, and I am more than willing to repeat this experiment in the future. The other day a Swedish YMCA representative visited the camp. We were allowed to talk to him, and he had basically got hold of all the law books I need. I will be receiving them soon. You don't need to send me any more books then. My studies are slowly progressing. We are all well, all healthy. I do hope the same goes for you. My regards to family and friends. Take care. Much love, Finn.

18/7—44

Dear father, mother, Emil and Rikke. Many thanks for the letter from mother, dated 12/6, from Emil 29/6, from Uncle Magnus 12/6, Ellen Harboe 16/6 and from Baarlid 12/6. They all came here on the 12/7, so Emil's letter only took two weeks, which must be a record. He did a great job getting an Mg [referring to the Norwegian grade system] in Latin, and I hope Rikke will also do as well. All is well around these parts, and we're feeling optimistic about the future. We have maps over our wall, and pay close attention to them. Take care, and my regards to all friends. Jan and Erling say hello. Much love, from Finn.

27/7—44

Dear Uncle Emil and Aunt Ellen! Many thanks for the letters dated 23 May and 4 June. I received them at the end of last month. It is very interesting to read about how you're doing, and very nice to receive the photographs you sent me. It is unfortunately not possible to get Norwegian newspapers, but we get the German ones each day, so we do pay attention. Everything's fine here, we're all healthy and well and in good moods. Say hello to Eva, little Ellen and Eli. Take care. Much love, from Finn.

28/7—44

Dear father, mother, Emil and Rikke. Many thanks for mother's letter, dated 15/6, which I received today. I also got a letter from Bibi of the same date.

Yesterday we received two food parcels from the Red Cross, which pleased us greatly. In my last card I wrote that I had not received a parcel since 17th of March. It is wrong, it should have said 14/4. I have to congratulate Emil and Rikke on the results for their exams. I think they were very good indeed, and even better considering the study environment they are in. I am very much looking forward to coming back home to you all, and start my law studies in earnest. When you next call Jan's mother, do wish her a happy birthday. He had his own birthday celebrations here. It's from Jan S. We're spending most of the time out in the sun when it's shining, which it does quite often. I was feeling energetic at the start of July, and studied quite a lot. The other day, our room played a football match against another barracks room. We won 4–3. The room that lost had to serve everyone in our room a cup of tea. We've had more challenges since then, and will play the next game on Sunday. Another form of entertainment is betting. People place bets on everything. The stakes are mostly chocolate, sometimes whole plates of chocolate. I myself have been pretty lucky and have a whole plate of chocolate to spare. Take care, my regards to family and friends. Jan and Erling say hello as well. Many greetings, Finn.

7/8—44

Dear father, mother, Emil and Rikke. Many thanks for your letters, father, dated 5/7 and 18/7, and yours mother, dated 5/7, yours Emil from Tyriholmen, dated 11/4. They have taken three weeks to get here, not a bad pace. On the 2nd of August I received my book parcels. They all arrived at just the right time, I only had about 20 pages to go of my last one, so this worked out quite well for me. We had a little tea-party on Monday. We celebrated a very rare anniversary. Hank, a Canadian in our room, had been a prisoner for four years. It's an anniversary I do not think there's any chance of me or Jan ever celebrating. We made a cake, and it tasted very nice indeed. We ate it in a hurry. I heard Emil and Rikke had a nice trip, and I hope you had a wonderful time at Gåsøen. We're doing just fine here. The weather is good, and our moods great. I have written to Lall several times, but if she has not heard anything, give her my regards. Take care. Jan and Erling send their regards. Much love, from Finn.

19/8—44

Dear father, mother, Emil and Rikke! Many thanks father, for your letters dated 31/7, 3/8, and yours mother 4/8 and yours Rikke 7/8. I have also received April and May's parcels from the Red Cross, so all is well now. A week ago I also received another parcel from the Danish Red Cross. It's the second one I got from Denmark. Aller was the sender. I wrote him a card, and thanked him for the parcel a while ago. I also wrote a letter to Jan G. yesterday, and thanked him for his letter dated 22/7. All is well here. I hope all is well with you too. Jan and Erling send their greetings. Much love, from Finn.

29/8—44

Dear father, mother, Emil and Rikke. Many thanks for your letter Emil, dated 13/8. It took a week to get here. I received it on the Sunday after it was written. This is truly a record. During the last month we've had great sunshine each day, so we've been spending most of the time outside. This is a great advantage to us, especially since two more guys are now living in our room. Our garden is a source of great pleasure to us, and now the tomatoes are starting to look good too. We've had about 30 pumpkins from the garden as well. They don't make for good eating, but we've made plenty of jam from them, and with some sugar and oranges, they taste considerably better. At the end of last week, an American film came to camp. We'd heard rumours about it for about three months. It finally came. It was shown once, and another screening was planned, but not long into the second screening the apparatus broke. No chance of getting it fixed either, so we had to settle with being told the rest of the film by those guys who had seen it the first time it ran. No harm done really, as it was a low grade film. There're rumours of another one coming in now. Skelly, one of the guys I've taught Norwegian to, received some Norwegian books today. One of them was 'Snow and Skis' with many wonderful photos from Nordmarka [recreational area north of Oslo]. All is well here. My regards to family, and friends. Jan and Erling say hello. Much love from Finn.

15/9—44

Dear father, mother, Emil and Rikke. We've had brilliant sunshine for two months now. We are all healthy and well in all ways. A loudspeaker has been mounted onto one of the barrack walls. We can now listen to [blurred handwriting] each day. They are listened to with great interest. Letters have been sparse lately. My regards to friends and family. Much love, from Finn. Jan and Erling send their regards.

18/9—44

Dear father, mother, Emil and Rikke. I write to you in English this time, because I think the Norwegian censor is away from some time, as we have not received any letters during the last four weeks. Today, Erling and I went for a two hours walk together with 28 officers and four German guards. It was the first time we had been outside the wire since we arrived here, so you can easily understand how much we enjoyed it. We have a new system here now, so we should be able to take a walk like that once every 10th day, which is a very good thing. There is also an excellent band show being shown every night. The band plays 6 or 7 popular tunes (Black Magic, Smoke Opts in Your Eyes, Bragel, etc) a few good and many less good jokes, and three very amusing sketches. That was about all, but it was very well arranged, and I think all of the 'Kriegies' liked it. I have read all the books you have sent me, and I am going through them once more. Erling got some books on 'Book-keeping' which I'm also reading, so I have enough books to read for the rest of my stay. Our tomatoes are getting ripe these days, and we have at least one each day. I hope you all are well and fit, and give you my regards to the rest of the family and friends. Jan and Erling send their regards too. Much love from Finn.

[Thus end the letters back home. At this point, the Russian Army was pressing ahead from the east, and western forces from the west. Finn still had a long way to go, and was about to experience one of the toughest winters of his life, before finally coming home in the summer of 1945.]

Endnotes

Chapter 8. A Temporary Fear of Flying

1. Giørtz, Fridtjof, *En Krigsflyvers Dagbok* (Oslo: Wings, 2000), p. 53. [*A Fighter Pilot's Diary*]
2. Hartmann, Harald, *Catalina mot Ubåt* (Oslo: Wings, 1998), p. 53. [*The Catalina versus the U-boat*]
3. Giørtz, p 60.

Chapter 9. Final Steps at Prince Edward Island

1. Hartmann, p. 60.

Chapter 13. B-Flight's Losses

1. Bjercke, Alf R., *Backup av et rikt liv* (Oslo: Dreyer, 2001), pp. 145-146.

Chapter 14. Hunting the *Lützow*

1. Skavhaugen, Knut, 'Marineflyger fra Elverum', *Flyhistorie*, 23 (2012).

Chapter 15. The Last Sortie

1. Giørtz, p. 180.

Chapter 19. Tunnelling

1. Read, Simon, *Human Game: Hunting the Great Escape Murderers* (New York: Constable 2013); Guhnfeldt, Cato, *Spitfire Saga V* (Oslo: Wings, 2014).